Oneness in suffering

Look at the painting on the front cover. What d
you? The artist, Theyre Lee-Elliott (1903-1988), pa
an illness in which he came close to death. With
came a deep desire to paint the crucifixion of
form of a dying tree. From childhood, he had so
resemblance between trees and human beings. Although an
agnostic, he was searching 'to find the point at which the
wood of the cross and the agony of Christ met', and he added
to this the symbolic strands of barbed wire from two World
Wars. Think of other symbols you might add in the light of
more recent events.

This year's prayers are a response not only to the destruction
of the World Trade Centre in New York but also to many parts
of the world where there is conflict and suffering.
Intercessory prayer is an attempt to share the suffering of
those for whom there is 'no easy peace': ordinary people like
ourselves who have become victims of war, oppression,
discrimination, HIV/AIDS, rejection ...

Cover image
Crucified tree
form – the agony
(tempera and
gouache 1959)
Theyre Lee-Elliott
Methodist Art
Collection
© Trustees for Methodist
Church Purposes

How to use this book

- As you pray, know that you are praying not only for but with
  those who are mentioned, or who have written the prayers.
- You may not have time to use all the material each day.
  Select and focus on different aspects and places each
  month.
- The meanings of the symbols are given on page 80.
- Use your newspaper and include the day's news.
- Use spaces in the margins to write the names of people
  who need your support.
- Use the Lectionary readings on pages 74-79.

God answers prayer

There may be no magic cure for many situations, but God
does answer these prayers: God's answer is usually a
challenge to do all that we can – personally, socially and
politically – towards the relief of suffering and for the peace
and harmony of all people and the earth itself.

Maureen Edwards

Prayer Handbook
Committee
Maureen Edwards
(Editor)
Susan Johnson
Michael King
Norman Wallwork
Sarah Middleton
Brian Thornton

Cover design
and layout
Lorna Lackenby

An outline for Morning and Evening Prayer

Open our lips, O Lord,
And we shall praise your name.
Glory to the Father, and to the Son,
and to the Holy Spirit:
As it was in the beginning, is now,
and shall be for ever. Amen

(From Easter to Pentecost: Alleluia)

Hymn *

Psalm * and *Glory to the Father*

Scripture *

Canticle from *Hymns and Psalms*

Morning		Evening	
S	825	S	826
M	833	M	828
T	824	T	831
W	832	W	829
T	831	T	830
F	829	F	644
S	830	S	832

The Lord's Prayer

Collect of the Day or of the Week

Morning Collect
Lord our God, as with all creation, we offer you the life of this new day; give us grace to love and serve you to the praise of Jesus Christ our Lord. Amen

Evening Collect
Lord our God, at the ending of this day, and in the darkness and silence of this night, cover us with healing and forgiveness, that we may take our rest in peace, through Jesus Christ our Lord. Amen

Thanksgiving

Intercession

The Grace

* See Lectionary

An outline for a Preaching Service

Welcome and Call to Worship

Hymn

Prayers:

　　Invocation or Adoration

　　Confession

　　Declaration of Forgiveness

　　Collect of the Day

Hymn

Old Testament Lesson

Psalm

Lesson from the Apostles (Epistle)

Hymn

Lesson from the Gospels

Sermon

Hymn

Prayers

　　Thanksgiving (for Creation, Redemption in Christ and the life of the Church in the Spirit);

　　Intercession * (for the Church and its mission; for the world and its communities; for the sick and those in need; specific petitions and remembrance of those who have died).

　　The Lord's Prayer

Notices

Offering and Prayer at the Offering

Hymn

Blessing and Dismissal

* Including relevant day in Prayer Handbook

No Easy Peace

Prayers from which to select for personal devotion or public worship

Praise

Lord of all, we praise you –
At the dawn of the day
and the setting of the sun.

Lord of all, we praise you –
For the energy of creation
and the diversity of cultures.

Lord of all, we praise you –
For your challenging presence
and the renewal of your people.

Lord of all, we praise you –
For your continuing light in Christ
and the love which makes us one.

Lord of all, we praise you –
For your empowering Spirit
and the strength to work for peace.

Lord of all,
May we praise you through our lives,
Honour you by our words,
And serve you with our neighbours
    across the world,
For the glory of your kingdom. Amen

Ian T White,
President of the Methodist Conference

Our dear Father,
in whom we live,
you are worthy of praise
and worship
from every creature,
from the rising of the sun
to its setting ...
In grace, you created the world
and in compassion you redeemed it.
Your might is beyond measure,
your wisdom beyond knowledge,
your love beyond telling.
We bless you for the gift of life,
for your guiding hand upon us,
and your sustaining love within us.
We bless you for Jesus Christ,
your Son, our Saviour,
for the living presence
of your Holy Spirit,
for your Church, the body of Christ,
for the ministry of the Word
and sacrament
and all means of grace.
Guide us, O Lord,
in all the changes of life,
that we may neither complain
in adversity
nor boast in prosperity,
but with faith, hope and love
follow your divine will,
through Jesus Christ our Lord. Amen

Isaac Mumba,
United College of the Ascension

Landscape Light
© Digital Vision Ltd

Confession

Loving God,
you have given us a diversity
of gifts to celebrate,
and to enrich our common life,
but we confess
that pride in our own ways
has separated us from our neighbours.
We recall with shame
the story of our past:
the prejudice and discrimination
which have marred our community,
the wars that have brought death
   and destruction,
and which deny the vision
of your Kingdom for all peoples.
God of all mercy,
Forgive us and heal us.

You have called us
to carry the cross -
to suffer, if need be,
for the sake of your Kingdom
of peace and justice,
but we confess that
we have taken the easy way:
when we were meant to listen
we talked of ourselves;
when we should have spoken out,
we were silent;
when we should have acted
we were paralysed by fear.
God of all mercy,
Forgive us and heal us.

Renew us with your Spirit
and set us free,
so that we may go out
to forge new relationships
and to work for justice
and harmony for all peoples,
as we follow the Prince of Peace,
Jesus Christ our Lord. Amen

Maureen Edwards

Prayers for peace

Dear God, you created one perfect world,
but we have divided it into different
groups. Help us to learn through your
Holy Spirit what you would like us to do in
a world now at war with itself, that we
may help you to restore its goodness.
You created us in your image, although
you made us different. Thank you for our
individuality through which we see your
all-inclusive love. Let us remember that
we are all important parts of your creation
and never feel ourselves superior or
inferior to anyone.
We pray in the name of Jesus whom you
sent to bring peace on earth and goodwill
to all people. Amen

Constance Magnus, Jamaica

God of all,
we pray for the world in which we live,
your world and ours,
a world in which there is
   no easy peace.
We recognise the anger and tensions,
between North and South,
rich and poor,
Christian, Muslim, Jew and Hindu,
black and white,
East and West,
Catholic, Protestant and Orthodox,
gay and non-gay,
young and old,
fundamentalist and liberal,
male and female.
Yet you are God of all, and call us
to work for justice, love and peace.
By your grace enable us to follow
   the vocation of the cross
which earths your love in our world
   and in eternity.
In the name of Jesus Christ. Amen

Peter Howdle,
Vice-President of the Methodist Conference

Eternal and ever loving God,
You have set us in a world of beauty
    and wonder
a rainbow people,
    one family under you,
yet with such richness and diversity.
In our fear and in our greed
We have turned away from each other
building up the walls that divide
and smashing the bridges that unite.
At this time we pray for peace,
even small moves towards peace,
In those areas ravaged
    and scarred by protracted war,
by costly and lengthy hatreds
    and violence.
We pray for the Holy Land,
for Sudan and Angola,
    Somalia, Sri Lanka and Colombia...
Strengthen the peacemakers
    and bring peace in our time, O Lord.

Jennifer Potter

Come, Holy Spirit,
fill us with love,
so that differences caused by economic
and social injustice may be removed.
Fill us with your Spirit of justice,
so that we can fight against poverty
    and exclusion.
Come, Holy Spirit, Giver of Peace,
use us in a world which is polarised, where
hostilities and violence
    have erupted between people
    and communities
    who were at peace
but who now distrust each other.

Harbinger of Shalom,
fill us with your Spirit of tolerance
    and solidarity,
so that mutual respect may be established,
in the name of Jesus Christ
who reigns with you
and the Holy Spirit. Amen

*John Mohan Razu, Bangalore,
India/United College of the Ascension*

'Peace be with you' *John 20:19,21*
Lord Jesus
    who said, 'Peace be with you,'
    to the disciples in their fear,
help us to receive your peace
    in our times of trouble
    when we know our need.
Lord Jesus
    who said, 'Peace be with you,'
    to the disciples in their joy,
help us to receive your peace
    in our times of happiness
    when we forget our need.

*Sheila Norris,
Mission Partner in Japan*

Closing prayers

Eternal and Gracious One,
through whom we live
    in a world of need,
here we have tasted your goodness,
and hungered for a world more just.

Though afflicted by pain,
    brokenness and division,
here we have heard your call
to be a people
    of healing community.

Though daily we touch our limits,
here we have received
    the treasure
of your unfailing grace.

Make us instruments of your peace,
abiding in faith,
    in hope and in love. Amen

God is with us,
Christ is calling us,
The Spirit will guide us.
We are not alone.
Thanks be to God.

*United Church of Canada Moderator's Day
of Justice, Healing and Reconciliation*

Africa

Secretary: Roy Crowder

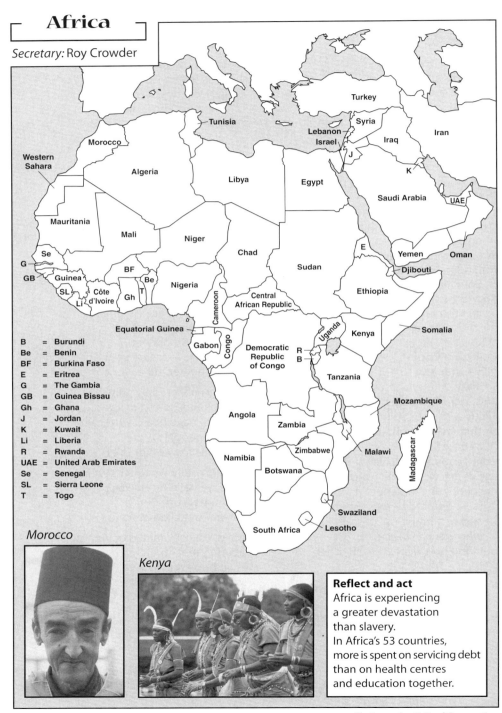

B = Burundi
Be = Benin
BF = Burkina Faso
E = Eritrea
G = The Gambia
GB = Guinea Bissau
Gh = Ghana
J = Jordan
K = Kuwait
Li = Liberia
R = Rwanda
UAE = United Arab Emirates
Se = Senegal
SL = Sierra Leone
T = Togo

Morocco

Kenya

Reflect and act
Africa is experiencing
a greater devastation
than slavery.
In Africa's 53 countries,
more is spent on servicing debt
than on health centres
and education together.

Photography © *Corel Corporation*

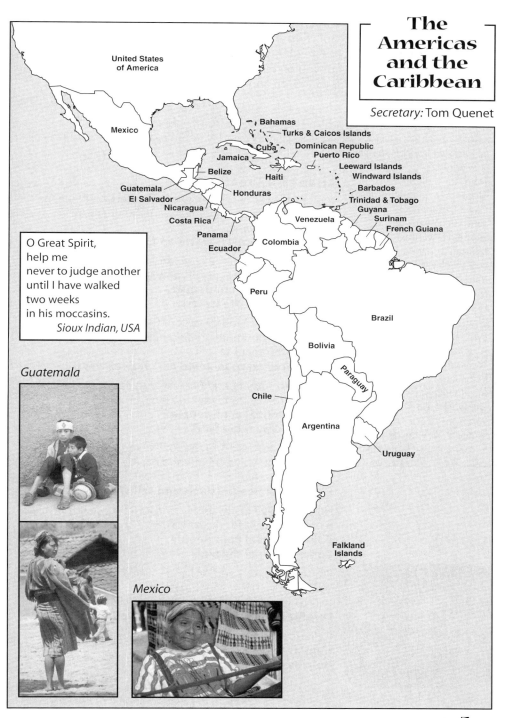

The Americas and the Caribbean

Secretary: Tom Quenet

United States of America

Mexico

Bahamas

Turks & Caicos Islands

Cuba

Dominican Republic

Puerto Rico

Jamaica

Leeward Islands

Belize

Haiti

Windward Islands

Guatemala

Honduras

Barbados

El Salvador

Trinidad & Tobago

Nicaragua

Guyana

Costa Rica

Venezuela

Surinam

Panama

French Guiana

Ecuador

Colombia

Peru

Brazil

Bolivia

Paraguay

Chile

Argentina

Uruguay

Falkland Islands

O Great Spirit,
help me
never to judge another
until I have walked
two weeks
in his moccasins.
Sioux Indian, USA

Guatemala

Mexico

day 1

Bless me, O Fountain of Life, with the gift of your Holy Spirit, that all that cannot live in your presence may be consumed by your holy love, until they come to fullness of life with you on earth and fullness of glory with you in heaven; for your truth and your mercies' sake. Amen

Philip Doddridge, 1702-51

Praying with the whole creation

Scholarship students studying in Britain:
John Ataya (Kenya)
Mntungwa Caba° (S Africa)
David Desai° (CNI)
John Gichimu° (Kenya)
Htay Kyi (Myanmar)
Morgan Kumwenda (Zambia)
Meresiana Kuricava° (Fiji)
Matere Muaror° (Fiji)
Heneli Niumeitolu
Benhur Pennaperuru° (CSI)
Roseneice Nogueira (Brazil)
Abedu Quashie° (Ghana)
Jeyakumari Ratnasingam° (Sri Lanka)
Maylin Richards (Belize)
Daniel Tannor° (Ghana)
Paul Sanki (CSI)
Iouliana Dresvina (Russia)
Yordan Zhekov (Bulgaria)

Litany for Creation

Praise to you, O God, source of all waters.
For vast oceans, flowing rivers, and gentle rains
we give you thanks.
Forgive our careless waste and polluting ways.

Help us to cleanse, conserve, and share;
teach us to care for the gift of water.
Come and heal your people.
Come and heal the waters.

Praise to you, O God, creator of the dry land.
For mighty mountains, rolling hills, and fertile paddocks
we give you thanks.
Forgive our wanton greed and violent ways.

Help us to sow, till, and harvest with care;
teach us to live gently on the land.
Come and heal your people.
Come and heal the land.

Praise to you, O God, breath of life and maker of air.
For wind and wave, breath and breeze, light and life
we give you thanks.
Forgive our heedless acts and selfish ways.

Help us to live justly, simply, and wisely;
teach us to care for the gift of air.
Come and heal your people.
Come and heal the air.

Praise to you, O God, Lord and Giver of Life.
Your love sustains planet earth
and by your hand all things living are fed.
Forgive our neglect and abuse of your gifts.

Help us to serve, defend and restore your creation.
Help us to care for your people.
Help us to care for the earth.

Paul Chalson, Tasmania
Prayer Handbook of the Uniting Church of Australia, 2002

Photograph by B Wolstenholme

Give thanks for the work of Development in Diversity Officers, helping to make the most of the opportunities presented to us by the diversity of our churches.

Pray for a new initiative in rural ministry in the Tendring area, and for churches throughout the District facing the challenge of adapting themselves for new ministries.

Our calling

Dear God,
how many calls there are:
the call of the wild birds,
the call of everything that is beautiful,
the call to be faithful,
the call to be myself.
From where do they come,
these beckonings of another world,
these wistful tuggings of my sleeve,
half regretful, never quite disregarded?
They are echoes of a greater calling
heard like a bell tolling on the far shore.
May I catch the sound of your divine call
through all the noisy clamour of things
and have the wisdom to follow,
even though you may lead us
along unquiet ways,
for in you is my peace,
but never an easy peace.

Nigel Collinson

God of peace,
you paid for peace
for us and for all people
for all time.
Help us not to demand
from others, or from ourselves,
the price of peace,
but to receive and share
your costly peace;
for your love's sake. Amen

Ermal Kirby

London North East District

Chair:
Ermal Kirby

Secretary:
Clifford Newman

President of British Methodist Conference:
Ian White

Vice-President:
Peter Howdle

Youth President:
Peter Barley

Women's Network President:
Caroline Salmon

Secretary of Conference:
Nigel Collinson

Assistant Secretary:
Keith Reed

Co-ordinating Secretaries:
David Deeks
Jonathan Kerry
Ruby Beech
Peter Sulston

Diaconal Order Warden:
Margaret Matta

Give thanks for the order and beauty of created things

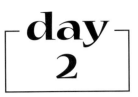

day 2

O Source and Centre of all being, grant us the gifts of your grace, that walking in your way and strengthened by your life, we may journey through this world in your peace, and rest in heaven with your saints; and this we ask through Christ our Lord. Amen

Gerhard Tersteegen, 1697-1769

 in West Africa (1)

The Gambia District

Chair:
Titus Pratt

Mission Partners:
p Robbie Bowen°
n Ruth Bowen
p Elaine Woolley°
ad John Woolley

Experience Exchange:
Emily John

Our Father in heaven, all praise and honour to your name.
May your kingdom come, in all its glory, in The Gambia;
release your people to preach your good news;
water this dry and thirsty land
that our lives may be fruitful for you
as the mangoes.
Inspire your Church as it moves towards autonomy.
Give wisdom to our Government.
Be our Teacher in the classroom
and our Doctor in the clinic.
May your will be done now and always.

Ruth Bowen

Sierra Leone

Methodist President:
Francis Nabieu

We pray with all who have suffered the trauma of war
    for lasting peace:
God's tender words of comfort and hope
are for all peoples.
God's glory is seen in the wilderness
and a voice cries out:
'Prepare the way of the Lord...'
God feeds his flock 'like a shepherd';
    he gathers the lambs 'in his arms'.
God, the Creator, whose love encircles all,
never wearies: God's understanding
and his solidarity with the most vulnerable
    are 'unsearchable'.
We pray with all who place their trust and hope in God
                that they may be renewed,

> Peace is not only better than war, but infinitely more arduous.
>
> *George Bernard Shaw*

able to rise up 'with wings like eagles'
to run 'and not be weary',
to walk 'and not faint'. Amen

Based on Isaiah 40

Give thanks for new members in several circuits;
for work with overseas and post-graduate students at Dublin Central Mission.
Pray for counselling services in Bray and Dun Laoghaire;
for asylum seekers and economic migrants, and for continued readiness to welcome them in worship and to provide for their distinctive needs.

Dublin District

Superintendent:
Thomas Kingston

Secretary:
R Donaldson Rodgers

Give thanks for the 35th anniversary of the Chinese congregation at Kings Cross and its continuing growth;
for the new Mission Partnership of five denominations in Milton Keynes.
Pray for Anne Brown, as she begins her new ministry in chairing the District;
for the asylum detention centre in Bedfordshire, its detainees and visitors;
for new ventures in mutual ministry with the Anglican Diocese in St Albans.

London North West District

Chair:
Anne Brown

Secretary:
Brian King

Mission partners:
Bernardino° and
Elizabeth Mandlate
(Mozambique)

Self-revealing God, accept the gift of each one's abilities.
Continue to challenge
and stretch us in our expectations
of what we may do and be in your service.
Enable us to serve the neighbour, the friend
and the newcomer.
May we have grace to meet Christ,
our welcoming Saviour, in each.

Thomas Kingston

*Photograph by
B Wolstenholme*

Lord of the great concerns and the everyday routine,
in the quiet of your presence,
we commit the day's activities to you.
Inspire giving and receiving in every conversation;
direct each decision;
give us strength when tempted to avoid difficult decisions –
    or people;
make us more aware of your Spirit at work beyond
our immediate horizons.
May every time of frustration, disappointment,
    weariness or pain,
bring us closer to the love you offer us in Jesus. Amen

Margaret Jones, Poulton-le Fylde

*Give thanks for
the resources of
the earth*

day 3

Praying with Christians in West Africa (2)

In your mercy, O Lord, may the oppressed find deliverance, may the helpless be defended and may the fallen be raised up. Support the needy, heal the sick and bring home again the outcast. By your grace may the hungry be fed, the weak strengthened and the captive brought to freedom, that together at the last we may rejoice as children of the same God and Father; through Jesus Christ our Lord. Amen

Clement of Rome, died c. 95 CE

Togo

Methodist President:
Matthias Creppy

Pray for this newly autonomous Church facing new opportunities and working out its mission;
for the work of 'La Bonne Semence' training centre offering tuition in practical skills to help women to become self-supporting.

Benin

Give thanks that the clinic at Porto Novo is now the Bon Samaritan Hospital, serving a very large area of remote villages: 'a dream come true'.
Pray with the All Africa Methodist Leaders' Conference for a strengthening of dialogue between the separated communities, for the healing of the wounds that keep them apart, and for the continuing partnership between the Methodist Church in Benin, the Methodist Church in Côte d'Ivoire and the Methodist Church in Britain.

Côte d'Ivoire

Methodist President:
Benjamin Boni

Mission partners:
n/m   Shirley and
   Yao Assandey
   N'Guessan, Stan,
   Geni and Rory

Give thanks for the enthusiasm of our young people and spiritual growth.
Pray for the opening of L'Institut Supérieur de Theologie d' Abidjan (ISTHA) in October;
for those going forward for training as ordained ministers;
that the mission of the Church will not be frustrated by financial difficulties.

Shirley and Yao Assandey N'Guessan

Call to repentance!

Companies in the UK have exported over £27 billion of armaments in the last five years. British weapons are used in most of the world's conflicts. In many countries children are trained to fight and kill, and are often used as targets and maimed by land mines. We are all responsible if we do nothing to stop this evil.

Pray for John Swarbrick as he begins his chairmanship;
for deepening ecumenical relationships;
for our universities and colleges;
for all engaged in the enterprise of Higher Education;
for students, teachers and support staff;
for chaplains and the opportunities of chaplaincy;
for Southlands College and its place in the University of Surrey Roehampton;
for the witness of the Methodist Church in **Gibraltar** which is part of this District.

London South West District

Chair:
John Swarbrick

Secretary:
David Chapman

Holy and eternal God,
we thank you for the gifts of mind and intellect.
Help us to live searchingly and to grow in knowledge and in our love of you and of all creation.

Robert Jones

Praying for peace – a hymn

God's on our side and God will grieve
at carnage, loss and death;
for Jesus wept, and we will weep,
with every grieving breath.

God's on their side, the enemy,
the ones we would despise;
God quench our vengeance, still our pride,
Don't let our anger rise.

God's on each side, God loves us all,
and through our hurt and pain
God shares the anguish, nail scarred hands
reach out – love must remain.

God show us how to reconcile
each difference and fear,
that we might learn to love again
and dry the other's tear.

*Andrew Pratt – Written on 12 September 2001
after the destruction of the World Trade Centre*

*Copyright © 2001 Stainer & Bell Ltd, London – Metre: CM,
Suggested tunes: Amazing Grace, Edgware, Gerontius, St Fulbert, University*

THE LEAVES OF THE TREE ARE FOR THE HEALING OF THE NATIONS

O God, make good that which is between us; unite our hearts and guide us into the pathways of peace.

A Muslim prayer

Give thanks for the gift of human life

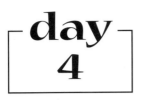

day 4

O Holy and Blessed Trinity, within the circle of redeeming fire cleanse our hearts, purify our souls and strengthen our wills. Fill us with your grace and overshadow us with your love that we may daily delight in your presence and glorify you alike in word and deed; now and for ever. Amen

Richard Rolle, 1290-1349

 in West Africa (3)

Equatorial Guinea

Methodist Lay President: David Prospero Sharpe

Give thanks for commitment in face of difficulty.
Pray for Christians who are victims of abuse and torture; for the renewal of the Church in this persecuted and forgotten nation.

Ghana

Methodist Presiding Bishop: Samuel Asante-Antwi

Mission partners: p/ed Alan° and Pam Harvey

Give thanks for the influence of Methodist schools and colleges and the part their leavers play in the life of the nation and the world.
Pray for this country and its Churches which face increasing financial problems;
for the HIV/AIDS awareness and care programme (funded by a World Church Grant), now seeking to help the many families whose lives are overshadowed by tragedy;
for Ghanaian communities in Britain, and that we may be enriched by their enthusiasm and strength of faith.

A meditation from Africa

Open your hand and think on God's grace. To you are freely given all the blessings of this life, placed in your open hand. The gift of this life, placed in your open hand. The gift of life itself; the love of parents; health and vigour of body; joy of friends; enrichment of education; all given into your open hand. Freely given is work, marriage, children. But now, because we are susceptible to this spiritual disease, when a gift is given, our reaction is to close the hand, to keep the gift so that it might not slip away. But just as surely as God gives, he comes to claim the physical things: a parent, a marriage partner, our work, our physical health, at last life itself. And when the hand is closed, God's taking back hurts us. But keep the hand open. For as surely as God comes to take back that which he has given, it is only so that he might give us a greater gift.

Procession of Prayers, Edit. John Carden (Cassell)

Give thanks for the growth of the Killarney Church and Charleville meetings, for new church workers in Shannon and Kilkenny, and for the contribution of those immigrating from other countries.

Pray for the success of the Power to Change programme, District-wide youth work, children's clubs, especially summer opportunities.

Children's club

Midlands and Southern District (Ireland)

Superintendent:
David Range

Secretary:
John Sweeney

Give thanks for the many new signs of exciting life throughout the District;

for unexpected opportunities for sharing the gospel, especially in South London, along the Thames Gateway, and in many other places;

for significant growth in ecumenical understanding.

Pray for an increase in love and desire for the rich variety of race and culture in our District;

for grace to celebrate our differences as gifts from God, especially in places of high tension and poignant memories of Damilola Taylor and Stephen Lawrence;

for a passionate love of justice and freedom from fear in all our relationships, after the impact of 11 September 2001;

for the witness of the Methodist Church in **Malta** which is now part of this District.

London South East District

Chair:
Harvey Richardson

Secretary:
Jeremy Dare

Our dancing God,
loving and moving God,
may your Holy Spirit dwell within me,
   that your love may fill my world;
help me to see the wonder and beauty of your presence
   in all things,
even when peace is uneasy or far away;
help me to weed the garden of my soul
   and root out the undergrowth,
the brambles and the weeds;
for then I will be free to grow, and free to love
as you are, in your dance together,
Father, Son and Holy Spirit. Amen

Harvey Richardson

Give thanks for creative vision and inventive skill

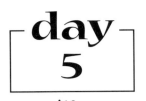

day 5

Lord Jesus Christ, Light of the World and King of Glory, help us to offer to you the gold of faithful worship and true devotion, the incense of constant prayer and adoration and the myrrh of suffering obedience and growing conformity to your holy and perfect will; for your truth and mercies' sake. Amen

John Tauler, 1300-1361

Praying with Christians in West Africa (4)

┌─ Cameroon ─┐

Moderator of the Presbyterian Church:
Nyansako-ni-Nku

Mission Partner:
th   Peter Ensor°

Give thanks for large, growing congregations.
Pray for the work of the Presbyterian Theological Seminary; for fully trained pastors leaving the Seminary to begin their ministry, each with about 1000 communicant members to care for; for wisdom for Church leaders in knowing how to care for congregations who have no pastor at all; for the Emmanuel Sisterhood at Bafut – the only Protestant monastery in West and Central Africa – for their care of orphaned and deprived children, including many refugees.

┌─ Nigeria ─┐

Methodist Prelate:
Sunday Mbang

Mission Partners:
sd   Ros Colwill
d   Hans and Mary
     Van den Corput,
     Marcel and Maurice
sd/m   Peter and Sarah
     Dockree (+CA)

Give thanks for Wesley Guild's continuing support for community health care in Nigeria.
Pray with all who are involved in the development of a medical clinic at Ado-odo (the latest project funded by Wesley Guild) – a region where malaria and other killer diseases abound; with all at Amaudo as work is now developed to help people with learning difficulties, offering support for families, special education and a day centre; for a similar new project (supported by a World Church Grant) in the Benue Diocese.

Lord, we praise you for Nigeria and her peoples;
for the land and its rich human and natural resources;
for a new democratic government.
Let peace, which passes human understanding,
be made known at all times in Nigeria.
May this year bring salvation from every form of bondage.
Turn our shame to glory, sorrow to joy,
hatred to love, violence to peace,
and may we see your presence in all our endeavours,
through Jesus Christ our Lord. Amen

Joshua Olukayode Adegun (Nigeria/UCA)

Give thanks for the work of Methodist Homes in Nuneaton, Leamington Spa and Stratford upon Avon, and the variety of NCH projects around the District.

Pray for Christina as she resumes the responsibility of chairing the District;

for new developments in the Birmingham City Centre, the Methodist/Anglican Schools in Frankley and Hawkesley and for all who are called to serve in education;

for the work of the Arthur Rank Centre in Stoneleigh;

for those whose ministry is in hospitals and prisons;

for Christians who work to build up good relationships with their Muslim neighbours.

Birmingham District

Chair:
Christina Le Moignan

Secretary:
David Easton

Mission Partners:
Florence Deenadalayan (CSI)
Stephen and Angela Mullings, Stephanie, Angelique and Georgiane (MCCA)
th Israel° and Leelal Selvanayagam, Arul and Ani (CSI)

The way of peace

Gracious God, we seek your peace;
not the evil peace of status quo, which
'defends unjust laws and nurses prejudice'
but the Shalom of peace with justice.

You have shown us in Christ that the evils
of poverty, racism, power politics and
might as right do not make for peace,
and do not enrich humanity.

By your Spirit, teach us to know that peace
is not a thing to possess, but a way of possessing;
not a resolution of strife, but a way of striving;
not a journey's end, but a way of journeying.

Holy God, in the way of Christ we see
love and faithfulness come together,
justice and peace embracing.
May we find in Christ the Way of Peace.

Norwyn Denny, Redditch

Reflect: Someday, after mastering the winds, the waves, the tides and gravity, we shall harness for God the energies of love, and then for the second time in the history of the world, we will have discovered fire.

Teilhard de Chardin (1881-1995)

Give thanks for God's care for people

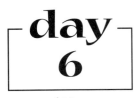

day 6

O God, most gracious, in your infinite pity, lead me to the gentle stillness of your glorious presence, where at the heart of the burning flame I might dwell unharmed and unconsumed, abiding forever in your love, forever redeemed and forever at rest; through Christ our Lord. Amen

Frances Ridley Havergal, 1836-1879

 in Southern Africa (1)

The Methodist Church of Southern Africa

Methodist Presiding Bishop:
Mvume Dandala

South Africa
Experience Exchange:
Michael Baxter
Elizabeth Belilios

Botswana

Lesotho

Namibia

Swaziland

Mozambique
Methodist Bishop:
Henrique Mahlalela

Mission Partners:
th/ed Peter° and
Janice Clark

Give thanks for richness of community and faith: that amid the struggle there are people of hope, hospitality and joy; for all who seek to unite people across ethnic divides.
Pray that we may learn from the Churches of Southern Africa what it means to be the 'Servant Church' in the context of wealth and poverty.

HIV/AIDS

Pray with all who are determined to make this year a turning point in the HIV/AIDS pandemic, South Africa's 'new enemy' (one in every five people carry the virus);
for all who are raising awareness and promoting a spirit of caring and compassion;
for HIV/AIDS care centres for children and adults;
for all who struggle to reconcile the need for condomisation with their Christian values of fidelity and sex within marriage.

Lord, we pray for a change of heart in the world
that will respond to those in greatest need.
We pray for your guidance
as we try to understand the HIV/AIDS pandemic,
and for our role in reducing its spread throughout the world.
Enable each of the nations
to clarify their role in trade policies,
so that fair trade may become a way of life
which will raise the living standards of the poor.
Give to your Church, we pray, the strength
to live your Gospel for the sake of the poor.
In the name of our Lord and Saviour,
Jesus Christ. Amen

Bernardino Mandlate,
Mozambique/North London

> We are not intimidated by what is before us, because we walk with God.
>
> *Mvume Dandala*

Give thanks for the increasing ventures in Creative Arts across the District and for the newly formed District Evangelism Team, seeking to equip churches to face the challenge of the future; for continuing links with South Africa, not least through our Methodist Primary Schools.

Pray for groups in Bolton, Bury and Rochdale, seeking to build closer relationships with other religious communities and sharing common concerns for the regeneration of society.

Bolton and Rochdale District

Chair:
Keith Garner

Lay Secretary:
Margaret Higson

*District Creative
Arts Contact*

Inter Faith relationships

Your love, Lord, flows without bounds
    throughout the universe,
holding in its
embrace women and men
    of all faiths and none.
We hold up to you a world
    fractured by inter-religious mistrust,
    fear and rivalry.
We pray for those places where differences of faith
    have caused violence or discrimination.
We bring before your love
    all who have suffered in such situations
and all who work for reconciliation,
building understanding where there has been fear,
and co-operation where there has been competition.
May that which can unite people of different faiths –
mercy, compassion and self-giving love –
cut through our differences
    so that we can work together,
in justice, courtesy and love,
    for a more peaceful world.

Elizabeth Harris, Secretary for Inter Faith Relations

Loving God, may we fulfil our calling as your people,
    finding new ways to declare the values of the
        Kingdom,
    experiencing your love with each other,
    and demonstrating your compassion to all who hurt.
In our weakness, remind us of all that you have done
    for us in Christ,
    and empower us with your grace.

Keith Garner

*Give thanks
for God revealed
in the prophets
and the
Scriptures*

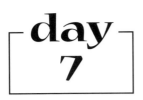

day 7

Grant to us, O gracious God, ears that are attentive to your word, eyes that are perceptive to your glory and wills that are ready to keep your commandments that with true and faithful hearts we may rejoice in your perfect will; through Christ our Lord. Amen

Christina Rossetti, 1830-1894

Praying with Christians in Southern Africa (2)

The United Church of Zambia

Synod Bishop:
Patrice Siyemeto

Mission Partners:
p   David° and Rhoda Nixon, Samuel and Christopher
ag   Jane Petty (+C of S)
ad/ad   Brian and Georgina Payne (+C of S)

Experience Exchange:
Betsy Lafferty

Give thanks for vitality of faith (almost 90% attend church), for national stability and potential;
for the Container Ministry of the Methodist Church in Ireland which is clothing orphans and providing resources for schools and clinics in Zambia.
Pray for families and churches coping with loss due to HIV/AIDS, and for orphaned children;
for all who are involved in the Life Skills programme – in partnership with Scripture Union Africa – training 'peer educators' for AIDS awareness in schools;
for the United Church, grappling with serious questions and needing to develop a plan for financial sustainability;
for the country as a whole facing serious economic problems: decreasing aid from donor countries and the knock-on effects of the 11 September attack in the USA.

Zimbabwe

Methodist Presiding Bishop:
Cephas Mukande

Mission Partners:
ed   Jonathan and Isobel Hill, Stephen and Susanna
p   Graham° and Sandie Shaw and Matthew
p   Clifford° and Ruth Taylor
rt   Pat Ibbotson

Give thanks for people of faith and courage.
Pray with prayer cells in Buluwayo South for healing for all the people, that justice, peace and righteousness may prevail;
that land reform may be implemented with due regard for human rights, and transparent democratic principles;
for prophetic leadership and for those who risk their lives by their stand for justice, truth, non-violence and peace;
for the vulnerable and unprotected;
for the dawning of a new day . . .
for each of our mission partners serving in difficult situations.
Zimbabwe has the highest HIV/AIDS rate in the world – one in four are infected. No family remains untouched.
Pray for those who experience rejection;
for the accessibility of cheaper drugs: that pharmaceutical companies may put compassion before huge profits . . .

Give thanks for the visionary shared work and witness of our two United (Methodist and United Reformed) Areas of Mid and West Wiltshire;

for the continuing challenge and stimulus to think ecumenically when planning outreach, mission and service.

Pray for the ongoing ecumenical and inter faith explorations with the Bristol City Council to develop shared project and community work;

for the effectiveness of the newly formed Bristol Black Churches' Council in representing and empowering black-led churches, especially in developing working relationships with white-led churches.

Bristol District

Chair:
Ward Jones

Secretary:
Carrie Seaton

Give thanks for steady work throughout this rural District in public worship, fellowship groups, children's and youth activities and Christian witness.

Pray that we will be a people of FAITH: followers of Jesus Christ, alert to people's needs, both overseas and at home.

Enniskillen and Sligo District

Superintendent:
Aian Ferguson

Secretary:
Philip Agnew

Lord,
Help me to create a 'God space'.
When that decision has to be made:
    Lord, what would your mind be?
When that meeting is to take place:
    Lord, what would you say?
When that action is to be taken:
    Lord, what would you do?
When that 'word in season' is required:
    Lord, is it really your word that has come to me?
Through what I say and do, enable those around me
to encounter Jesus at their point of need.

Ward Jones

God of Peace, our Creator and Redeemer,
you have brought to us peace through our Lord Jesus Christ.
Make us gentle to everyone.
Keep us from being anxious about anything,
help us to ask you and trust you for what we need,
with thanksgiving.
Let your peace guard our hearts and minds
in Jesus Christ our Lord. Amen

Aian Ferguson

Give thanks for God's supreme revelation in Christ

day 8

Give to us, O Lord, the love that casts out fear, the faith that seeks your presence, and the trust that leans on you in all adversity and temptation, and grant that loving, believing and trusting we may come at length to the joys of your eternal kingdom; through Jesus Christ our Lord. Amen

Louisa M Alcott, 1833-1888

Praying with Christians in East Africa

Kenya

(Tanzania and Uganda)

Methodist Presiding Bishop:
Zablon Nthamburi

Mission Partners:
th/m Michael° and Heather Chester
n Barbara Dickinson
sd/d Paul and Rachel Lindoewood, Hannah and Michael
d Claire Smithson
d/n Dietmar and Birgit Ziegler, Nora, Samuel, Ronja and Jacob (+EMK)
th Caroline° and Andrew Wickens, Matthew and Catherine (+CMS)
d David and Mary Sarson

Give thanks for the growing number of students at the Methodist University in Meru, and for qualifications now offered in theology, Christian education and counselling, business, agriculture, biology, applied mathematics and computer studies – all contributing to Kenya's growth as an industrial nation.

Pray for **Time travellers**, the Methodist Children's Project.
As we hold in our minds:
    children with no family,
    children in single-parent families,
    children whose parents cannot afford to educate them,
    children whose parents have died of AIDS,
    children on the street, children foraging for food ...
we pray for Methodist nursery and primary schools in Nairobi and Meru,
for children sponsored by the Karibuni Trust and other agencies, children given hope for the future;
for teachers working with little equipment;
for the vocational training project at Kariokor;
for those who are working with families, helping them to improve their quality of life so that their children do not end up on the streets;
for all who serve in situations where it's hard to see how things will ever change ...

Pray for a positive outcome to the trial of a new AIDS vaccine being carried out in partnership by the universities of Nairobi and Oxford;
for the AIDS Awareness programme;
for the Methodist Church at Machungulu which has started a health centre to provide home-based care for neighbours and friends suffering with AIDS;
for outreach and evangelism in Northern Kenya, Uganda and Tanzania;
for all who lead this Church in difficult times.

Give thanks for the faithful witness of churches in rural communities, towns and seaside resorts;

for churches where both English and Welsh are used, and for new projects being pioneered in some circuits;

for the growing number of Local Ecumenical Projects.

Pray for the Inter Faith Council formed by leaders of the National Assembly, the Amelia Trust Farm and its work with excluded young people;

for rural communities where young people move out to seek employment and others move in to retire, that our churches may be seen as relevant and caring;

for a new vision for churches of all denominations as we seek a way forward together, so that Wales will once again be blessed with spiritual renewal.

O God, in all our confusions about the future of Methodism, empower us with your reconciling love that crosses boundaries and breaks down walls. May your love permeate our lives and churches so that we may build your kingdom of truth, justice and love.

Barbara Bircumshaw

Arglwydd Dduw, cymorth ni i fod yn barod i newid;
i newid ein hagweddau, ein gweledigion, ein hymdrechion.
er mwyn i ni adnabod anghenion ein gilydd a 'r byd.
Cymorth ni i fod yn groesawgar i 'r rhai sy 'n symud i 'n plith.

Loving Lord,
enable us truly to share each other's pain.
Reassure us in our efforts as we seek to do your will
and to fulfil your mission.
Continue to challenge us to be a Church
that takes risks in the name of the One
who took the greatest risk of all time.
We pray that every hamlet, village and town in Wales
will rediscover its spirituality and interdependence:
a love and desire for communities to live at peace.

Eluned Williams

South Wales
Chair:
William Morrey

Secretary:
Jack Healey

Cymru
Chair:
Patrick Slattery

Secretary:
Dennis Griffiths

North Wales
Chair:
Barbara Bircumshaw

Secretary:
Paul Nzachahayo

Y Gymanfa:
Y Llywydd:
Chwaer Eluned Williams

Secretary:
Alan Hall

Treasurer:
Anthony Gregory

Amelia Trust Farm

*Give thanks
for the obedience
of Christ to the
Father's will*

23

day 9

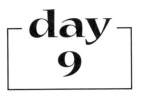

O Holy Spirit, giver of light and life; impart to us thoughts higher than our own thoughts, and prayers better than our own prayers, and powers beyond our own powers, that we may spend and be spent in the ways of goodness and love, after the perfect image of our Lord and Saviour Jesus Christ. Amen

Eric Milner-White, 1884-1963

Praying with Christians in South America (1)

Brazil

Bishop:
João Alves de Olivera
  Filho

Uruguay

President:
Adolfo Tomé

Argentina

Bishop:
Nelly Ritchie

Mission Partner:
p   Sueº Jansen

Colombia

Bishop:
Isaras Guttiérrez

Ecuador

President:
Salomon Cabezas

Give thanks for followers of Jesus Christ,
preaching his Word: the prophetic announcement
and action in solidarity with a world where uncertainty
and violence hinder its peoples from living the peace
and hope of the God of Life.

Adolfo Tomé, Uruguay

Pray for wisdom to minister in a society which is increasingly troubled by crime and drug trafficking …
for all who work with street children in **Brazil**.
Pray for growth in commitment and number in **Uruguay**;
for ministry among an increasing number of excluded people: adolescent mothers, street children, the unemployed and homeless; for the task of consoling families whose young people have emigrated in search of work;
and for people who suffered the floods in 2002.
Pray for democracy in **Argentina**: for Churches who are calling upon politicians to put an end to corruption, impunity and the abuse of power;
for new congregations of vision seeking to express the love of Christ, and for new outreach projects led by Pastor Eduardo Morales (National in Mission) and Pastor Mario Perez in the town of Pacto in **Ecuador**.

Lord, we confess our sins before you. Our hearts are discouraged by doubt and sorrow. We are too weak to share the good news of the living Christ. Our bodies and spirits are torn apart by war and injustice. We fervently long for your Breath of Life to be infused in us, so that we can proclaim the power of your resurrection and the victory of abundant life above any project for death. Lord, break the chains, untie the bonds, make us one in you so that we can proclaim the end of this era of death and show to all the world the Life that abounds in you. Amen

Horacio Mesones, Colombia

Give thanks for people who, in the face of disaster, have dared to believe that God is love;

for people who are working through experiences of hurt and are determined to make a fresh start without anger and recrimination;

for people who are sensitive to the needs of their neighbours.

Pray for ministers in single stations, and for our commitment to maintain and create an effective Christian presence in villages; for new ways of being church and for creative and generous ways of using slender resources.

Cumbria District

Chair:
David Emison

Secretary:
David Andrews

Arising

Lord,
I feel the dawn rising
In my heart
As the touch of your love
Waters the dry places
Of my life
And new growth begins.

Still I am clasped
By the night
But the darkness
Which threatened
Is vanishing before
The gentle coming of the dawn.

Landscape Light
© Digital Vision Ltd

Lord,
Help me to rise
With all your disciples
In this city;
Help us to share
In your resurrection
And the new life
You offer for the world.

Generous God
in your mercy heal us
in your grace renew us
in your power enable us
and in your love give us to
    your world
for Jesus' sake. Amen
David Emison

Brian Frost
Prayers of Darkness and Light
(New World Publications)
– written in the long period when he
suffered from ME

*Give thanks
for the value
Christ gave to
human labour*

day 10

Make us diligent, O Lord, in our duties, watchful against all temptation, and pure and temperate in our enjoyment. Help us never to transgress your royal command to love our neighbours as ourselves, and grant that loving you above all else we may be preserved blameless at the coming of your Son, our Saviour Jesus Christ. Amen

Thomas à Kempis, 1379-1471

Praying with Christians in South America (2)

Bolivia

Bishop:
Carlos Intipampa

Give thanks for the influence the Methodist Church – though small in number – has had on the life of Bolivia;
for large numbers of adherents, a strong youth movement and active women's groups.
Pray for all who are involved in leadership training to ensure that Christians are well grounded in their faith;
for the work of CLEM which is developing community health care centres and education for women, and which encourages them to reflect creatively on their situation and discover how they can help themselves;
for the Second Mile project which is providing bilingual text-books for schools;
that the participation of indigenous peoples will become a more integral part of the nation's life.

Peru

Bishop:
Marco A Ochoa

rt   Margaret° and
   Aldo Valle

Give thanks for church planting and new mission in the Cuzco area.
Pray for the development of the right kind of theological training for ministers and for those ministers serving in rural areas where churches are growing but where resources are too scarce to provide adequate stipends;
for the Church's witness in matters of human rights.

Chile

Bishop:
Pedro Grandón

Dear Lord, we thank you for the beautiful and diverse country of Chile, its warm people, peace and stability.
We continue to pray for forgiveness and reconciliation to heal the wounds left deep in the lives of many during the Pinochet years;
for the unemployed and the growing economic gap;
for Chile's ethnic minorities and that there may be mutual respect and a peaceful solution to the problems of the Mapuche communities;
for the Church's spiritual growth and the mission of planting new churches and building manses.

Kathryn Thomas and the Liturgy group, Concepcion School

Give thanks for the faithfulness of ministers and lay people in worship and witness throughout this widespread cross-border District.

Pray that with the shortage of ministers available to serve in circuits, people may discover and accept their role for ministry in the local church.

North West District (Ireland)

Superintendent:
Ian Henderson

Give thanks for Methodist Homes in the Channel Islands: Stuart Court, Maison La Corderie and Maison L'Aumone.

Pray for and commend to God's gracious keeping those who live and work in them and all who in so many ways support these centres of care;

for the work of ACET, teaching English to members of the Portuguese community and promoting community relations in Jersey;

for the Guernsey Council of Churches' work of reconciliation, strengthening bonds of friendship and encouraging exchanges with the churches and schools of Biberach, to which many islanders were deported in the 1940s.

Channel Islands District

Chair:
Ian White

Secretary:
June le Rossignol

Lord, your patience with human weakness is endless
your love for me is from everlasting to everlasting
and your commitment to your creation is eternal.
By your Holy Spirit,
enable me to persevere in the face of discouragement.
Fill me with a love that is unconditional.
Help me to make my commitment to you
and to your Church, not just for today
but for all the remaining days of my life.

Ian Henderson

Loving God, when the storms blow,
and the waves crash upon our lives,
we fear that we may sink under the weight of our anxieties, and our courage melts away.
May we find you alongside us in the unfathomable deep,
through him who rebuked the wind,
stilled the sea and offers us your peace, Jesus Christ.

Ian Suttie, Guernsey

Give thanks for the strength Christ gives to his disciples

day 11

O God, from whom to be turned is to fall, to whom to be turned is to rise, and in whom to stand is to abide for ever: grant us in all our duties your help, in all our perplexities your guidance, in all our dangers your protection, and in all our sorrows your peace; through Jesus Christ our Lord. Amen

St Augustine, 354-430 CE

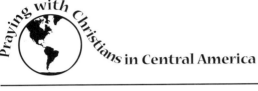 Praying with Christians in **Central America**

Belize and Honduras District
of the MCCA

District President:
David Goff

Give thanks for mission in a multi-cultural community, for God's work in challenging and surprising ways.

Pray for ministry to people with HIV/AIDS (55% of Central America's AIDS population is in Honduras) – for parents and grandparents grieving the loss of their 20-30 year-old generation and caring for orphaned children.

Panama and Costa Rica District
of the MCCA

District President:
Lesley Anderson

Almighty God, give us strength in times of weakness and vision in our blindness. We cry to you as we wrestle with problems of unemployment, family disintegration, substance abuse, prostitution and violence.

Despite our problems, we give special thanks for your Son, our Lord Jesus Christ; for evangelistic and missionary outreach in Sol Naciente, for schools in every circuit, for dedicated and committed members, and for all who pray for us and help us in our time of need.

Lesley Anderson

Guatemala

President:
Juan Pablo Ajanel

Pray for the country still recovering from 36 years of armed conflict, with scarce resources and unemployment;

for CEDEPCA, organising courses for women in church, in prison and for those damaged by the 1980s ethnic cleansing, so that they can become self-supporting.

Mexico

Bishop:
Antonio Aguiña
    Márquez

We pray that we may faithfully fulfil the mission entrusted to us by our Lord Jesus Christ wherever, by his grace, work has been established;

for children and young people, that they may have a personal experience of Jesus Christ;

that the love of God may bring hope to the underprivileged;

that God may greatly bless the Methodist Church family in every continent, so that we may be the light of the Lord shining in the darkness.

Antonio Aguiña Márquez

Give thanks for the service given to many denominations and the wider community by the Methodist Book Centre in Hanley, with space for Traidcraft and a counselling service.

Pray for continued good inter-faith relations with Muslim communities in Stoke-on-Trent and the work of the liaison officer between the churches and city council;

for volunteers at St Peter's Ecumenical Church Centre, Chester, welcoming visitors to the city;

for the relevant programmes of learning together which are being developed by the Training and Development Group;

for the unique work of Englesea Brook Chapel and Museum providing coach-loads of school children with a memorable day's experience of schooling in the costumes and style of yesteryear but with values for today.

Chester and Stoke on Trent District

Chair:
John Walker

Secretary:
David Scott

Towards Church unity

Gracious God,
we thank you for the rich diversity of your Church;
for your people who celebrate,
through worship and service,
the beauty of your love as revealed in Jesus.
Forgive our prejudice and all that divides;
forgive our arrogance and all that hurts.
In our disunity weave our broken strands together
and give us the vision of what your Church could be,
not for our own sake, but for your world.
In Christ's name. Amen

Stuart Burgess, York and Hull District

THE LEAVES OF THE TREE
ARE FOR THE
HEALING OF THE NATIONS

Lord of the Pennine Peaks and the Cheshire Plain,
help us to perceive and love you in many ways:
in the quietly understated and the stunningly impressive,
when our gaze goes out and we focus in;
at times when we are more than fully stretched
and moments when we rest in the familiar.
One thing we ask: that we may not be dull,
for glory crowds and beckons us on every side –
the hovering heights and widening plains of love
in Christ the Lord. Amen

John Walker

Give thanks for the call to follow Christ

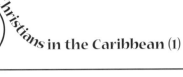

day 12

Eternal God, as you have made us for your glory let us magnify you with both body and soul, with both our thoughts and our intentions, and with both our words and our actions, and grant that, having undertaken our whole life for your praise, we may enter hereafter into the joy of your eternal presence; through Christ our Lord. Amen

Jeremy Taylor, 1613-1667

Praying with Christians in the Caribbean (1)

Methodist Church in the Caribbean and the Americas (MCCA)

Connexional President:
Bruce Swapp

Pray for the life and mission of the MCCA, 'a Church in full sail on troubled waters';
for all who make plans to deal with hurricanes.

Dear God, the waters that wash the shores of our islands remind us that your Spirit is moving over our region.
As your Son called people who made a living by the waters to follow him, so may we hear your voice beckoning us to serve you.

George Mulrain – (Transmission USPG 1999)

Guyana District

District President:
Barrington Litchmore

Give thanks for enthusiasm and commitment.
Pray that the momentum created by the Bicentenary of Methodism in Guyana may lead to a deepening of faith and to new initiatives in mission.

Leeward Islands District

District President:
Selwyn Vanterpool

Give thanks for the District's new theme: 'Called to share your faith'.
Pray that every congregation may be a centre of evangelism and that each member may hear and respond to the call to share his/her faith with others;
for lapsed members;
that God's presence may be welcomed in every home.

South Caribbean District

District President:
Victor Job

Mission Partner:
p   Elaine Thomas °

Give thanks for active evangelism, workshops on family life and class leaders' training programmes.
Pray for those who are involved in developing programmes to deal with drug abuse, violence and HIV/AIDS;
for the Church's influence in family life and society where there is a breakdown in law and order;
for Bible study groups and prayer meetings;
for dialogue between people of different faiths in Trinidad.

Give thanks for congregations who help and support members of the farming community in difficult times, and for the work of Roger Greene (District Agricultural Chaplain) who continues to be a listening ear to many.

Pray for all who are unemployed or who struggle on low wages, and for the wise use of European Objective One funds, so that long-term benefit might be seen in our many areas of great poverty; for good relationships between local people and itinerant individuals and groups who come to Cornwall for flower picking and other seasonal work.

Cornwall District

Chair:
Chris Blake

Secretary:
Howard Curnow

Mission in Britain

God, thank you for the many ways in which faith is shared:
for those who seek to make the good news of Jesus Christ relevant to the variety of cultures in Britain today;
for those planting new churches –
some that look like traditional churches,
others that we find hard to call 'church' at all;
for acts of love and service which provoke people
into asking 'why?';
for good news shared using every form of media;
for District Evangelism Enablers
and all who equip churches to look outwards.
Help us to share the calling of the whole Church
to proclaim Christ confidently in word and deed;
to long for our friends and neighbours
to become followers of Jesus Christ;
to be church for those who don't yet belong.
In Jesus' name. Amen

New Media

Graham Horsley, Evangelism and Church Planting Secretary

Lord Jesus, meet with me today:
in my darkness,
meet with me as Light;
in my uncertainty,
meet with me as Vision;
in my loneliness,
meet with me as Friend;
in my anxiety,
meet with me as Peace. Amen

Chris Blake

Give thanks for opportunities of work and leisure

31

day 13

Grant us, O God, reverence as we remember your glory, penitence as we remember your holiness and gratitude as we remember your love, that we may go from strength to strength all our days with our knowledge deepened, our love rekindled and our hope re-awakened; through Jesus Christ our Lord. Amen

William Barclay, 1907-1978

 **Praying with Christians in the Caribbean (2)**

Jamaica District

District President:
Philip Robinson

Mission Partners:
p/p Conrad° and
  Sonia° Hicks, Nathan,
  Olivia and Nyasha

Heavenly Father, help us to accept into our lives your Son Jesus Christ who befriended sinners and outcasts, those whom others despised. Give us courage to challenge systems which create outcasts or encourage their existence.

May your Holy Spirit lead us into ways of caring for all, especially those whom others reject, those not appreciated by leaders of church or society, those who are discriminated against because of race, sex, culture, or lack of status. In the name of Jesus, friend of sinners and outcasts we pray. Amen

Constance Magnus

Bahamas and Turks and Caicos Islands District

District President:
Raymond R Neilly

Give thanks for growing political stability.
Pray for Derek Browne, a National in Mission, developing community work in Andros;
for the healing of the rift in the District;
for all who are working with social issues: HIV/AIDS, drug addiction, violence and crime.

Haiti District

District President:
Raphael Dessieu

Give thanks for areas of significant church growth and a strong sense of mission.
Pray for areas where the climate and work are hard;
for an end to the spiral of violence and injustice;
for the one million Haitians living in the Dominican Republic, many reduced to begging; for all who work with them, setting up feeding programmes, health services, education and legal advice to help them obtain citizenship, residence visas and work permits;
for families forced to flee from Haiti which is losing people with the best skills and education, and for the Church which has a vital role to play in this situation.

Give thanks that in a number of circuits Alpha courses are run jointly with people from many Christian traditions working together.

Pray for an end to sectarian hatred and violence;
for all who are seeking to break down the barriers of hate and suspicion.

North East District (Ireland)

Superintendent:
Paul Kingston

Secretary:
Roy Cooper

Give thanks for those involved in training and development, enabling people to grow in Christ and make the most of their gifts.

Pray for those working with people seeking asylum in Redcar, Middlesbrough, Stockton and Darlington;
for the new mission enabling team, seeking to encourage churches to fulfil their role in God's mission to the world;
for circuits responding to the need to work with fewer ordained ministers by re-focusing ministry with lay workers, and developing more flexible relationships with other circuits and denominations, especially Crook and Willington, Spennymoor and Ferryhill, Darlington and Cleveland.

Darlington District

Chair:
Graham Carter

Secretary:
Ian Scott

Peacemakers in the world

Lord, there must be times when you despair of humankind.
We don't seem to be able to work for peace
　　without using more violence.
War is used to combat war, hatred to combat hatred;
and then we express surprise when it doesn't work.
Jesus' way of accepting pain caused by others
as a way of loving and giving life
doesn't seem to be applicable to political, national
　　and international situations,
but the reality is that no-one dares give it a try.
At least help us to follow that way
　　in our personal relationships,
so that those who are different from us,
and those we would call enemies,
may find a welcome that opens the door to reconciliation.
So may we learn not just to pray for peace,
but to be peacemakers in the world.

Graham Carter

Give thanks for the truths God has enabled humanity to discover

day 14

O Lord God, when you give to your servants to endeavour any great matter, grant us to know that it is not the beginning, but the continuing of the same to the end, until it be thoroughly finished, that yields the true glory; through him who, for the finishing of the work before him, laid down his life, even Jesus Christ our Redeemer. Amen

Francis Drake, 1543-1596

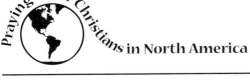

Praying with Christians in North America

United Methodist Church (USA)

Ecumenical Officer to the Council of Bishops:
Sharon Zimmerman Rader

Loving, creating and sustaining God, as we seek your guidance for us, we lift up to you the leaders of our nation, that they will be mindful of the call to your prophets of old, to seek peace, to use restraint, and to resist the temptation to yield to war.

Lord God, in this time of tragedy, we look for someone to blame. May we refrain from the rush to judgement by accusing all our Islamic sisters and brothers of being terrorists. Rather, may we be moved to reach out to them and to provide for them sanctuary as they attempt to live normal lives in our midst. Gracious God, may we heed your Word of love, peace, grace and wisdom as we seek to be faithful followers of Jesus Christ in these difficult times. Amen!

Melvin G Talbert, USA

The United Church of Canada

General Secretary:
Virginia Coleman

We pray that someday an arrow will be broken –
    Not in something or someone –
    But by each of humankind,
To indicate peace with one another, not violence.

Someday, oneness with creation,
    Rather than domination over creation and created beings,
Will be the goal to be respected.

Someday fearlessness to love
    And to make a difference will be experienced by all.

Then the eagle will carry our prayer for peace and love,
    So that all communities can sit in the same circle
    To communicate in love,
    And experience the presence
    Of the Great Mystery in the midst.
Someday can be today for you and me. Amen

From the Worship Service for the Moderator's Day of Justice, Healing and Reconciliation

http://www.uccan.org/airs/liturgy011104.htm
See also: http://www.uccan.org/healing.htm

Give thanks for the opportunity to spread information through the Internet, breaking down barriers that divide and helping people to grow in Christ.

Pray for the community of Polish people who live in Ipswich, and for asylum seekers living in Great Yarmouth and Kings Lynn; for English Language students who are exploited by the Gang Master system that operates in the Fens.

East Anglia District

Chair:
Malcolm Braddy

Secretary:
Grahame Lindsay

Mission Partners:
Frank° and Gabi
Aichele (Germany)

People at work

Creator God,
we pray for people at work:
those who know their work is creative
and those who see no purpose in it;
those who work uncomfortable hours
so that we may be comfortable;
those whose work takes them far from home
and those who are always bringing work home.

We pray for Workplace Chaplains:
give them sensitive spirits to know when to listen
and when to speak;
give them the insight and courage needed by prophets;
give them an awareness of your Spirit
when all around seems hostile.

We pray for our churches:
that our worship may hear the cries from the workplace;
that our caring may embrace those who find no work;
that our evangelism may stretch to those who work
beside us.

John Ellis
Secretary for Business and Economic Affairs

Workplace Chaplain

We thank you, God, for change and loss,
for experiences of decline which allow new ministries
to emerge,
and for challenging opportunities to create new futures.

Malcolm Braddy

Give thanks for the intercession of Christ in heaven

Asia

*Secretary for Asia and
the Pacific:*
Christine Elliott-Hall

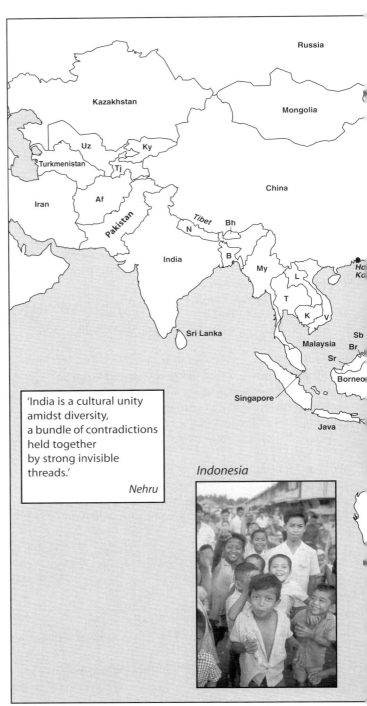

Russia

Kazakhstan

Mongolia

Uz

Ky

Turkmenistan

Tj

China

Iran

Af

Pakistan

Tibet

Bh

N

India

B

My

L

Ho
Ko

T

K

V

Sri Lanka

Sb

Malaysia

Br

Sr

Borneo

Singapore

Java

India

'India is a cultural unity
amidst diversity,
a bundle of contradictions
held together
by strong invisible
threads.'

Nehru

Indonesia

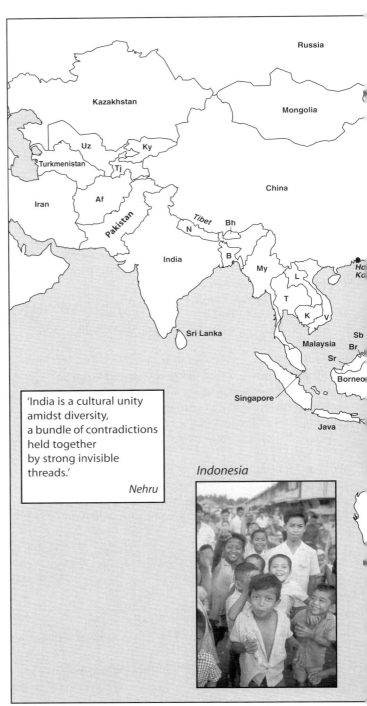

Uzbekistan

Fiji

Tonga

Samoa

Af	=	Afghanistan
B	=	Bangladesh
Bh	=	Bhutan
Br	=	Brunei
K	=	Kampuchea
Ky	=	Kyrgyzstan
My	=	Myanmar
N	=	Nepal
NK	=	North Korea
L	=	Laos
Sb	=	Sabah
SK	=	South Korea
Sr	=	Sarawak
T	=	Thailand
Tj	=	Tajikistan
Uz	=	Uzbekistan
V	=	Vietnam

NK

SK

Japan

wan

Philippines

Irian Jaya

Papua New Guinea

Solomon Islands

esia

East Timor

Fiji

Samoa

New Caledonia

Tonga

Australia

Aotearoa/ New Zealand

G is for grace and giving
O is for openness
D is for devoted

*Louise Poole (age 13),
Uniting Church of
Australia*

day 15

Grant, O God, that we may live in your fear, die in your favour, rest in your peace, rise in your power and reign in your glory, for the sake of your Son, Jesus Christ our Lord. Amen

William Laud, 1573-1645

Praying with Christians in the Middle East

Israel/ Palestine

Jordan

Lebanon

In peace, let us pray to the Lord,
that the grief of those who mourn, and the memories of those who cannot forget past hurt, whether Muslim, Jew, or Christian, may be healed by God's loving touch;
that across all barriers of race and creed, we and all who dwell in our land may respect each other's dignity and seek to serve each other in love:
Let us pray to the Lord: **Kyrie Eleison** (Lord, have mercy)

That our self-interest and self-concern which have increased our neighbour's bitterness against us may be forgiven;
that the barriers of hatred, suspicion, anger, greed and fear may be removed from our hearts and minds;
that all who are now in conflict in our land may renounce violence and seek peace:
Let us pray to the Lord: **Kyrie Eleison** (Lord, have mercy)

That the Holy Spirit may lead us from prejudice to truth and mercy, teach us to love our enemies, and deliver us from hatred and vengefulness;
that we may commit ourselves to establishing true peace and reconciliation in the unrelenting search for justice and a world order that is fair to generations yet to be;
that swords may be hammered into ploughshares and spears into pruning knives, so that wolves and sheep live together in peace:
Let us pray to the Lord: **Kyrie Eleison** (Lord, have mercy)

Sabeel Liberation Theology Group, Jerusalem

Pray with people throughout the Middle East who are powerless against those who threaten them, the bereaved, orphans and refugees;
for small communities who need to be held together;
for the rebuilding of home and community life;
for Christian Aid and other relief workers;
for the healing of all wounds, for peace ...

Pray for Grace Easthope, the new minister at Peel in the Douglas Circuit, and for the full-time appointment to the Castletown Circuit of Kath Corkish;

for Lys Vaughan, the new lay worker at Kirk Michael in the Ramsey Circuit;

for the Tercentenary Celebrations following the footsteps of John Wesley across the Island;

for the development of the work of the Manx Live at Home Scheme, MHA.

Isle of Man District

Rheynn Ellan Vannin Yn Agglish Haasilagh

Chair:
Stephen Caddy

Secretary:
Irene Robinson

Prayer for prisoners

Father God,
With you, we remember all who are in prison.
For those made hard and cynical by life 'inside';
for those who feel no sorrow for the crimes
    they have committed;
for those who today are contemplating further crime –
send your Spirit of truth.

For those who create anxiety and fear;
the weak who are abused by the strong;
and those who never receive a letter or a visit –
uphold them in your love.

For those whose faith in Christ is mocked;
those who are taunted for going to Chapel;
those who today will respond to your word –
keep them in the faith.

Lord, forgive us for the silence that
    condones injustice,
    withholds forgiveness,
    disguises and fears,
    prolongs quarrels,
    breeds misunderstanding,
    shows contempt,
    permits ignorance,
    kills love,
    expresses indifference,
    increases fear
    and makes barriers.

Alan Ogier, Superintendent Chaplain of Prisons

Inmate with Chaplain
Photo © K E Photographics

Give thanks for the joy of human love and friendship

day 16

Lord God, the light of the minds that know you, the life of the souls that seek you and the strength of the wills that serve you; help us so to know you that we may truly love you, and so to love you that we may fully serve you, whose service is perfect freedom; through Christ our Lord. Amen

Gelasian Sacramentary, 8th Century CE

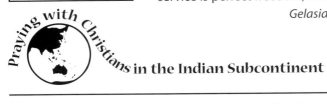

Praying with Christians in the Indian Subcontinent

Church of Bangladesh

Moderator:
Michael Baroi

Mission Partners:
n   Gillian Rose
th/ad+ Andrew and
    Rosemary Symonds
p+ Anne Tuesley
(all joint appointments
with CofS, CMS, USPG)

Give thanks for people of amazing warmth, generosity, skill and resourcefulness.

Pray with Christians who are a tiny minority (0.3% of the population), feeling more vulnerable and insecure since the bombing of Afghanistan, that their faith may be strengthened to withstand all difficulties;

for mission partners, that in wisdom and love they may be able to minister to people who can do little to improve their situation;

for the work at St Andrews Theological College as students prepare to serve in ways that will be costly;

for the steadily growing lay training programme and adult literacy work;

for the work of CSKS (funded by MRDF and helped by the MAYC Streets Apart project) which provides legal support and vocational training for destitute children;

for child-care programmes in slum areas, work in hospitals, schools and clinics;

for political stability.

Church of Pakistan

Moderator:
Samuel R Azariah

Give thanks for faith in adversity.

Pray with small Christian communities and NGOs who are acutely aware of how vulnerable they are to violence from extremist groups following the bombing of Afghanistan;

for small, scattered, poor communities who are keen to offer help to refugees;

that we and the people of Pakistan may recognise the solidarity of faith which transcends religious differences;

for a constructive dialogue of reconciliation with the world of Islam;

for the place of women in both Church and society and for all who work to improve their quality of life.

Give thanks for the continuing work of Oxford Place Children's Centre – a District Network Project – as it cares for the children of those attending the nearby Leeds Crown Court and Magistrates Court as defendants or witnesses.

Pray for the Harrogate Circuit as it engages in a major exercise to discern its future strategy and mission;

for the Night Light project in Wakefield, seeking to offer care and to share faith with the city's clubbing scene.

Leeds District

Chair:
Michael Townsend

Secretary:
John Santry

Give thanks for the witness of the Church, particularly in North Belfast, as it continues to be a 'sign of hope' for a real peace in a divided and often violent community.

Pray for the Rev Ivan McElhinney as he takes up his new responsibility as District Superintendent;

for each society within the District that they might have fresh inspiration and renewed strength to bring gospel values to our hurting city.

Belfast District

Superintendent:
R Ivan McElhinney

Secretary:
David Mullan

We pray for all seeking and administering justice:
for judges, magistrates and clerks;
for barristers, solicitors and advocates;
for people awaiting trial and their witnesses;
for the police, prison officers, probation officers
    and welfare workers –
that justice with mercy and common-sense may prevail,
that those who bear responsibility may know God's
    presence daily
to enable them to share his love with those who need it.

Roger Course, Dawlish

God of mercy and grace,
    you are endlessly patient with us in our weakness
        and failure.
May your acceptance of us, declared to us in Christ,
liberate us to love you and each other
and to offer you the radical obedience which faith requires;
We ask this through Jesus Christ your Son. Amen

Michael Townsend

Give thanks for our families and friends

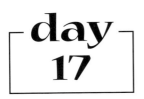

day 17

Grant to us, O God, in all our doubts and uncertainties, the grace to ask what you would have us do, that the Spirit of wisdom may save us from all false choices, and that in your light we may see light, and in your straight path we may not stumble; through Jesus Christ our Lord. Amen

William Bright, 1824-1901

Praying with Christians in India

Church of North India (CNI)

Moderator:
James Terom

Give thanks for the resilience of people living normal lives again after the earthquake in Gujarat.

Pray with Dalit communities struggling for recognition and for sustainable development which combines global and local knowledge;

for the massive quake-resistant housing programmes funded by Christian Aid in Gujarat;

for religious freedom and tolerance.

Remembering the heightened tension between India and Pakistan over Kashmir, pray for all who hold power in India that they may use it for the good of all.

Church of South India (CSI)

Moderator:
K J Samuel

Mission Partners:
sd   Margaret
     Addicott
p   Eileen Thompson°
(+CofS, USPG, CMS)

Experience Exchange:
Glenys Dykes

Give thanks for vision and a strong sense of mission.

Pray for the Association of Community Movements for Social Action (ACMSA), a community-based organisation to enable development in Dalit villages, equipping people with knowledge and skills;

with girls who are being helped to develop a more positive self-image.

Dear God, we praise you
for you have guarded and guided us these last 55 years
as Christians of different traditions have become one
for your glory.
We seek your gracious presence
as we strive for peace and justice,
especially for the sake of the Dalit communities.
Open our eyes to see people of all colours, all faiths
and all castes as they were created – in your image.
Help us to respond to our fellow human beings
without prejudice but with your divine love,
so that the marginalised are lifted up
as they are in your Kingdom for whose coming we pray.

Wilson Solomon, CSI/UCA

Give thanks for Epworth and the Old Rectory, the home of world Methodism, in this 300th Anniversary year of the birth of John Wesley.

Pray for the circuits of historic Lincolnshire as we celebrate our Wesleyan heritage, and explore new ways of being church;

for Peter Pillinger, our new District Mission Enabler, and the work of the Regeneration Team;

for the strengthening of the work of the Lincolnshire Rural Stress Network and the Lincolnshire Farmers' Support Group, as creative solutions are discovered and healing listening is offered.

Lincoln and Grimsby District

Chair:
David Perry

Secretary:
Christopher Humble

Photo © Arthur Rank Centre

For the vulnerable

All people are precious to you, our creator God.
So our prayers echo for the vulnerable ones of Lincolnshire.
Steel workers in Scunthorpe, farmers and farm workers
    leaving the land in their hundreds.
A quiet revolution? A creative work force silenced.
All people are precious to you, our healing God.
So our prayers resound for sexually assaulted women, men,
    and children,
The thousands of young who commit self-harm each year,
Isolated persons with mental traumas
    and unresolved dilemmas …

Alan Robson, Agricultural Chaplain

Challenging God,
    because we are all welcomed, accepted and loved,
    grant us strength to hold the vision
of making your church
a place where your welcoming love is felt
by the lonely, the abused and the unlovely;
a place where we nurture your embracing peace
    for all children,
even when they are not still or quiet;
a place where we can explore your accepting peace
    through different ways of naming you;
a place where we all feel uplifted, refreshed
and renewed, ready to go out and share your peace
with everyone we meet. Amen

Caroline Salmon, President of Network

Give thanks for the peace of God which passes all understanding

day 18

Lord Jesus, who stretched out your arms of love on the hard wood of the cross that all might come within the reach of your saving embrace; grant that we, stretching out our hands in labours of love for one another, may rejoice together at last in our knowledge and love of you; for you live and reign with the Father and the Spirit, one God, now and for ever. Amen

Charles H Brent, 1862-1929

Praying with Christians in Asia (1)

Myanmar/ Burma
The Methodist Church of Upper Myanmar

Methodist President:
Hao Khojam

Give thanks for a people of joy and delight, generosity and a strong evangelical faith.

Pray for Christian communities banned from meeting in buildings of less than 100 years old, and for those Christians who have gone into hiding;

for the Methodist Church and ourselves that we may be able to develop new ways of partnership that are less dependent on money;

for the deeply committed group of young lecturers working with few resources at the Tahan Theological College;

for the work of the Tahan Clinic, serving a very wide area and for people living in more remote areas without access to medical care;

for the Myanmar Council of Churches and its pastoral training, lay training, education and HIV/AIDS programmes.

Nepal
The United Mission to Nepal (UMN)

Director of the UMN:
Jennie Collins

Mission Partners:
Paul and Sarah Wright and Jack

Give thanks for commitment and courage.

Pray for Nepali Christians facing persecution from Maoist terrorists;

for peace talks between Government and Maoist leaders;

that peace will be restored and for all who lost loved ones in the conflict;

for wisdom for the UMN management team and for those who help them to know how to respond to threatening situations;

for the safety of UMN staff, uncertain of the future except that they are held by the love of God.

Reflect: **This will be a better world when 'the power of love' replaces 'the love of power'**

Give thanks for 'Our Calling',
with its challenge to open our eyes and clear our vision.
Pray for the Merseyside Churches reviewing their life together
that their common commitment may be renewed;
for CARE (Churches Action for Racial Equality) – working under
the auspices of the Churches on Merseyside –
and for its Director Hyacinth Sweeney-Dixon;
for those struggling to find new patterns of ministry;
for the Chair-Designate of the Liverpool District and his wife as
they prepare for new challenges.

Liverpool District

Chair:
John Taylor

Secretary:
Neil Stubbens

Struggle with cancer

O God of the open road,
in the last six months the way has been hard,
and we have not been easy companions.
I have travelled through shock and pain,
depression and anger, anxiety and loss;
while you have come and gone,
now close in the touch of nurses,
and the prayers of friends,
then leaving me to turn the corner of my fear,
or leap the gap of unknowing on my own.
But I thank you
for the generosity of your silences,
and for the patience of your withdrawal
while I have struggled with the Word
I could only hear when I stood alone.
It is awesome, and offensive:
startling, yet consistent with all that I know of you,
that even if I die of this,
even as I, daily, die through this,
my cancer is the gift of your endless and eternal love.
For me.

Photography
© Corel Corporation

© Julie M Hulme

Give to us, O Lord,
the peace of those who have learnt to serve you,
the peace of those who are glad to obey you,
and the peace of those who rejoice in your praise,
through Christ our Lord. Amen

St Aidan (d. 651)

*Give thanks
for our share in
Christ's ministry of
reconciliation*

day 19

To God the Father, who first loved us, and made us accepted in the Beloved; to God the Son, who loved us, and washed us from our sins in his own blood; to God the Holy Spirit, who sheds the love of God abroad in our hearts: be all love and all glory for time and for eternity. Amen

Thomas Ken, 1637-1711

Praying with Christians in Asia (2)

Sri Lanka

Methodist President:
Noel Fernando

Mission Partners:
lib Margaret Julian (+USPG)
p/m Davidº and Sue Palmer
ed Martin Stebbing

Give thanks for the cease-fire on 23 February 2002 giving hope for the future;
that the Methodist Church is fully involved in the peace process and rehabilitation programmes.
Pray with all who seek a permanent settlement of a conflict which has seen 60,000 deaths as the Tamil Tigers have fought for a separate homeland;
for the Methodist Peace and Reconciliation Committee which organises workshops, exchange programmes and youth camps between Tamils and Sinhalese;
for the Murunkan refugee camp – supported by the Methodist Church, the Government and NGOs;
for a deepening compassion, warm human relationships and a growing sense of unity ...

Indonesia and East Timor

Gereja Methodista
Bishop:

Give thanks with the Timorese people for Independence from Indonesia.
Pray that this fragile peace may be strengthened as justice is established;
for an end to sectarian violence in Indonesia;
for victims of gross human rights violations ...

Torture
We pray with people tortured by those in power – officials, police, the military –
in so many parts of the world.
People unjustly arrested, detained, beaten, given electric shocks, deprived of sleep,
set up for mock executions ...
people bruised, broken and traumatised ...
Loving God, you made us one family:
show us how to care and to use all possible ways to seek their freedom.

Give thanks for the work of chaplains in hospitals, prisons, universities, colleges, schools, residential homes and in industry and commerce.

Pray for the Inter-Faith Forum set up in Oldham as one of the responses to the racially motivated riots there last year; for the partnership between Anglican, Methodist, Moravian and United Reformed Churches in the Droylsden Churches on the Edge project in East Manchester;

for the proposed town centre chaplaincy to the retail trade, shoppers and residents in Ashton-under-Lyne.

Manchester and Stockport District

Chair:
David Willie

Secretary:
Frederick Bell

Photography
© Corel Corporation

In the shelter of God's wings

Hen-like God,
you surprise us with your awakening act
of immeasurable compassion and love.
You hatched us, injected life into us
and your Spirit brooded over us.
You formed us so mysteriously, and marvellous
is the rest of your creation that surrounds us.
You nurtured us with the warmth of your love
and the touch of your embrace.
When we stray towards dangerous predators,
you signal to us that we may rush back
and look out upon the world
through the feathers of your wings.
When you encourage us to go out,
your eyes watch over us.
You feed us by sharing what you have gathered
and reserved for us in your store.
When we encounter another of your broods
of different colours and looks,
let us not push them aside nor look indifferent,
but make them welcome,
creating a space for each of them.
Fill us with the joy of fellowship and enthral us
with your constant loving care and welcome
within the shelter of your wings.
Joining the host of your children, past, present
and future, we say Amen, Amen, Amen.

Leela and Israel Selvanayagam (CSI), Principal of the
United College of the Ascension, Birmingham

Give thanks for all who are agents of Christ's compassion

day 20

s in Asia (3)

Accept our gratitude, O God, for the goodness we have received at your hands and our joy at the continuance of so many mercies. Accept our penitence for the transgressions we have confessed and our thanksgiving for the pardon we have received. Bless the hearts given to you in unending devotion and the lives offered to you in endless praise; and this we ask through Jesus Christ our Lord. Amen

John Donne, 1572-1631

Singapore

Methodist Bishop:
Robert Solomon

We give thanks for the continuing witness of the Church in Singapore and throughout the region; for political stability and the social and religious harmony in our country.

We pray for the general ministry of the Methodist Church in Singapore, our 14 Methodist schools and units of our Methodist Welfare Services which care for the poor, the needy, the sick, the aged, the disabled, the imprisoned, and all those who require support in coping with their responsibilities and problems;

for the Methodist Missions Society and our missionaries who are serving faithfully in five countries – Thailand, Cambodia, Vietnam, China and Nepal;

for continuing ethnic and religious harmony, and peace in Singapore;

for the workers who have been retrenched during the recent economic downturn.

Robert Solomon

Malaysia

Methodist Bishop:
Peter Chio Sing Ching

Special assignment:
th   David and Rhona
    Burfield

Give thanks for political stability and harmony in this multicultural and multi-faith nation; for the rapid growth of the Church – the result of local Christians sharing the good news.

Pray for wisdom and sensitivity as Christians continue to share their faith;

for the training of pastors and church workers;

for a balanced proclamation of the gospel which brings wholeness – spiritually, physically, emotionally, mentally and socially;

for clear and relevant biblical teaching in the churches.

Cambodia

OMF Mission Partner:
Naomi Sharp

Give thanks that the foot-and-mouth crisis is over – that cattle populate the fields of Northumberland and Co. Durham again – and for the care that the farming community has been offered from our rural churches.

Pray for the work of the West End Refugee Service, Chatshop and churches in Newcastle as they offer welcome, advice and support to the many refugees and asylum seekers moving into this area; for the Mind the Gap project in the Gateshead and Jarrow circuit, creating church for the 20-40 age-group through Alpha, Cell groups and contemporary worship; for team leaders Elaine and Stephen Lindridge and all who work with them, and especially for those coming to faith and growing within it.

For Mission Partners

God of love and grace,
We thank you for all those who respond
To your call to serve overseas.
We thank you for all those who are
Willing to receive as well as to give,
And we pray that you will continue to
Challenge and encourage us
With your great commission,
'Go to all peoples everywhere
And make them disciples.' Amen

Alison Driscoll, World Church in Britain Partnership Co-ordinator

Give thanks for all opportunities to proclaim the gospel

Loving God,
In the tides that ebb and flow
we glimpse your faithfulness.
In the scars that mar our countryside
we feel your pain.
In the varied life of our towns and cities
we see you at every turn.
Help us to know that wherever we are,
you are beside us,
and at each time and place help us to declare
your purpose of healing, grace and love
made known in Jesus Christ our Lord.

Leo Osborn

Newcastle Upon Tyne District

Chair:
Leo Osborn

Secretary:
Elizabeth Edwards

Mission Partners:

Sipho° and Zime Nyembezi, Nkululeko, Nondumiso, Nosipho and Nokwazi (MCSA)

Hendry° and Rita Ponniah, Ian, Ruth and Roy (Malaysia)

Mind the Gap cell group

day 21

Praise be to you, all gracious God, that out of your goodness and loving-kindness, our fears have been turned into joys, our sighs have been transformed into song and our tears have given way to smiles. Amen

Anne Bradstreet, 1612-1672

 **Praying with Christians in the Far East (1)**

China

President of China Christian Council:
Cao Shengjie

Amity staff:
Ian Groves

Amity teachers:
Eileen Brodie
Richard Brunt
Stuart Craig
Mick and Anne Kavanagh
Richard Lester
Jody and Michelle Marshall
Mark McLeister
Vera Vicente

Amity is a Chinese non-Government Organisation founded by Christians

Hong Kong
(Special Administrative Region of China)

Methodist President:
Li Ping-Kwong

Picture to right:
Chinese papercut

Give thanks for the work of the Spirit among people of great commitment, and for crowded, growing churches;

for the work of the United Bible Societies and the Amity Printing Press, able to celebrate the legitimate printing of over 25 million Bibles;

that there is a Bible distribution centre in every province and that Bibles are being sold in many places;

for Amity teachers who are building bridges between China and their own people;

for Second Mile Projects which are helping to raise the quality of life in some rural areas.

Pray for the healing of past experiences which still hurt;

for Amity facing new challenges to meet the needs of poorer areas;

for the Church in its need to train more ministers to raise the quality of pastoral care, preaching and teaching;

for the development of a contemporary Chinese theology and that we may learn from China's insight;

for those who come to study and work in Britain and for the congregations who welcome and care for them.

Give thanks for growing confidence in **Hong Kong's** relationship with mainland China.

Pray for the Hong Kong Christian Council as it works to build closer links with the China Christian Council;

for new ventures in partnership with other Churches including the Methodist Church in Britain;

for the continuing work of the Methodist Centre offering after-school care for young children, rehabilitation for young offenders and support for older people.

'Teach us reciprocity as our rule of life; that we may not do to others those things we wish others not to do to us.'

A Confucian prayer

Give thanks for signs of growth and encouragement, especially for the newly opened Trinity Church in the South Ribble Circuit with all its opportunities to share the gospel.

Pray for churches seeking to bring hope and renewal to communities torn apart by tragedy and conflict:

for those who are building bridges between people of different races and faiths in the former mill towns of East Lancashire;

and for those who continue to work in the rural communities in the aftermath of foot-and-mouth disease.

North Lancashire District

Chair:
Stephen Poxon

Secretary:
Andrew Horsfall

Lancashire Farm
Photo by B Wolstenholme

Give thanks for growing church communities and exciting outreach among young people.

Pray for mission and evangelism throughout the District; for the Link project in Newtownards, combating delinquency and drug addiction.

Down District

Superintendent:
Robin Roddie

Secretary:
Thomas Deacon

Universal Prayer for Peace

Lead me from death to Life
from falsehood to Truth

Lead me from despair to Hope
from fear to Trust

Lead me from hate to Love
from war to Peace

Let Peace fill our heart,
our world, our universe.

Satish Kumar, member of the Jain community

This prayer was adopted by the Prayer for Peace movement, 1981. Join people of all Faiths who use it daily at noon.

In the stresses and complexities
in the violence and tension
in the unknown and unexpected
in our anxieties and fears
still our hearts and minds
to experience your peace.
Fill us with your Spirit of love and grace
and empower us to be your presence
in our world.

Jane Cullen, Scholarship Co-ordinator

Give thanks for the presence and power of the Holy Spirit

day 22

Teach me, O Lord, to use all my disappointments for the enrichment of my days. In each of the calamities that befall me let my heart be ever more closely knit to yours. Separate my affections for the lure of worldly things and set my soul in pursuit of true happiness and felicity; for the sake of Jesus Christ. Amen

Susannah Wesley, 1669-1742

Praying with Christians in the Far East (2)

Japan

General Secretary of the Kyodan, the United Church of Christ in Japan:
Shiro Harada

Mission Partners:
ed   David and Keiko Gray, Elizabeth and Paul
ed   Sheila Norris
ed   Daniel and Yasuko Dellming, Momoko and Daisuke

Give thanks that, although the Christian community in Japan is a tiny minority, there is faithful witness and testimony to God's presence and power, through worship, education and social work;

for those who are drawn to learn more about the Bible and to ask questions about the Christian faith.

Pray for the staff and administration of the theological colleges, that they may have wisdom and vision in training ministers to meet the needs of their congregations in Japan's changing society;

for the church-related schools and colleges, that the programmes that are developed may provide both good education and effective witness to Christ's love, and that the seeds that are planted may be nurtured and grow.

Sheila Norris

Korea

Presiding Bishop:
Kwang Young Chang

Mission Partner:
th/ad   Elinor Gordon° (+CofS)

Gracious God, we bring before you the people of Korea. We give you thanks for the Methodist people in South Korea as they prepare in hope for peaceful reunification with the North, and for the prosperity evident in the capital Seoul.

We commend to your care those struggling to survive as the drift from rural areas continues and farmers strive to repay their debts as the cost of rice falls.

We ask your blessing on those who work for justice, especially Korea Church Women United and our mission partner Elinor, that her work may in turn be a blessing, and the light of Christ shine ever more brightly, for we pray in his name. Amen

Beryl Cowling, Network President 2001/2

Give thanks for the work of Harrowby Lane Church, Grantham, among young people who misuse drugs and alcohol and among families on the surrounding housing estate who – because of the work of many committed people – have come to see the gospel in action.

Pray for the increasing number of homeless people and asylum seekers and refugees in Derby and Nottingham;

and for people who make up faithful, rural congregations who face fast-changing patterns of community and are endeavouring to live up to their calling with meagre resources.

Nottingham and Derby District

Chair:
Wesley Blakey

Secretary:
Averil George

Mission Partners:
Alexander° and Emily Siatwinda (Zambia)

God's perspective

Where we now are
is holy ground;
at every turn
God will be found.
In every breath,
in every word,
whispers of God
are to be heard.
Among the phantoms
of scorn and bite -
affirming Spirit
infinite.

He is the ground
of every life
and spectres, ghosts
and every strife
that haunt the soul
will always be
seen by his grace –
perspectively.

Wesley Blakey

Praise God who calls us and others to a full life;
Praise God who gives us this day to pursue it;
Praise God who forgives us for half-lived lives;
Praise God who opens new ways, doors
    and opportunities in life.
Praise God! Amen. Alleluia!

Leao Neto, Brazil/London

Give thanks for the ministry of the word, the sacraments and prayer

day 23

Govern our minds, O Lord, with your wisdom and our hearts with your infinite grace. Do not reward us according to our foolishness but after the manner of your great mercies, and as you have called us into the fellowship of your kingdom so may we live for ever in the light of your goodness and loving-kindness; through Jesus Christ our Lord. Amen

Teresa of Avila, 1515-1582

Praying with Christians in Australia and New Zealand

Aotearoa/ New Zealand

President:
Norman West

Give thanks for this land in which peace and security are accepted as birthrights and where races can intermingle while learning to respect each other's heritage.

Pray for the Church and for individual members as they develop skills to counter the endemic violence of a world which has lost its way.

Gracious God,
Your love is stronger than hate and greed,
Your grace is greater than injustice and suspicion,
Your hope can sustain us in a tortured world,
Your joy can transform us,
Your peace is needed by a world in pain.
We ask that you will enable us to share your Spirit's love,
grace, hope, joy and peace with all people.

Norman West and Heather Walls (Vice-President)

The Uniting Church of Australia
(UCA)

President:
James Haire

Loving God,
undiminished by distance,
unconstrained by place or time,
forever seeking, forever calling,
forever drawing humanity
to yourself and to each other,
we glimpse your spirit
in the brooding silence of awesome landscape,
the ancient law of Aboriginal nations,
the unspoken trust of honest mateship.
Yet in the vastness of this place, Australia,
we often feel alone, alienated, unworthy
of more than a passing acquaintance with your love.
Help us to understand
you ever yearn to make us whole,
drawing near in Christ
to show us the way.

Brian Smith, Gift of Grace, UCA Mission Prayer Handbook 2002

Give thanks for a growing vision of God at work in the city centre, for a deepening understanding of the work of God in village and town, and for faithful people giving themselves to God's work of 'turning sorrow into song' in the name of Christ.

Pray for asylum seekers and refugees, and integrity in all our relationships that there may be justice;

for ecumenical relationships and partnerships with other faiths, seeking new ways to serve and witness in our diverse communities;

for courage to face the hard decisions as we seek to respond to God's invitation to us to be made new.

Oxford and Leicester District

Chair:
Alison Tomlin

Secretary:
Martin Wellings

As your children, dear God

help us to love each other as you love us.
Show us how to love and value ourselves as you do.
Help us to see the best in ourselves that you see
and not to be surprised to see it in others.
Help us to forgive each other as you forgive us.
Help us with our foibles
before we turn them into virtues that distort our judgement.
Help us with our discernment,
particularly when we know the cost.
Give us the courage, dear God, to care more about
your will and being your child
than any earthly affiliations
no matter how beguiling.

Ruffo Bravette, Director of the Racial Justice Training Unit

Waking up this day, I smile.
Twenty-four hours before me.
I vow to live fully in each moment,
and look at all things with the eyes of compassion.

Thich Nhat Hanh,
Vietnamese
Buddhist monk

Living God,
yearning for all creation
to know the justice of your peace,
with your compassion, heal us;
by your truth, challenge us;
in your mercy, set us free;
in the name of Christ.

Alison Tomlin

Give thanks for our baptism and our call to serve Christ

day 24

Gracious Father, let us not address you with our lips when our minds are still far away. Let us not profess our love for you when our hearts are far from you. When we draw near to you in prayer may our spirits be at one with your Holy Spirit, and our longing for you be at one with that love through which you have saved the world; even your Son our Saviour Jesus Christ. Amen

Jane Austen, 1775-1817

Praying with Christians in the Pacific (1)

Pacific Conference of Churches (PCC)

General Secretary:
Valamotu Palu

Give thanks for the heritage and values of the Pacific culture.
Pray for the developing place of women in Church and society; that theological research may inspire social and political action and enable people to participate in the struggle for a more just society;
for a growing trust between people of different faiths;
for the support of the international community in issues of pollution and environmental catastrophe.

United Church in Papua New Guinea

Moderator:
Samson Lowa

Mission Partners:
t John and Jenny Willetts, Daniel and Peter (+ Wycliffe)

Give thanks for vitality of faith and worship.
Pray for the Church's ministry through clinics and hospitals and for those who are involved in developing an AIDS/HIV awareness programme (the AIDS epidemic here is reaching African proportions);
for political stability and the healing of memories of the Bougainville conflict;
for politicians making decisions which affect the future of rain forests which are in danger of eradication.

United Church of the Solomon Islands

Moderator:
Philemon Riti

Mission Partners:
ad Roger and Connie Cann

Give thanks for strong island communities holding on to traditional, religious and social values.
Pray for the United Church as it struggles to fulfil its mission with limited financial resources;
for the staff of the Helen Goldie Hospital as they explore ways of replacing old equipment and refurbishing wards;
for all who seek to protect their forests from excessive logging.

In what we share, let us see the common prayer of humanity.
In what we differ, let us wonder at the freedom of humankind.

Jewish prayer

Give thanks for the love and loyalty of those who give expression to the gospel of Jesus through the worship and work of the Church in small rural communities and deprived urban areas.

Pray for the three Methodist Independent Schools (Edgehill, Queens, Shebbear) and one day school (Watchet) in this District;

for chaplains, staff and students in universities and colleges of higher education;

for lay and presbyteral chaplains to industry, prisons, the Forces and the elderly;

for our many lay pastoral assistants;

for the new Chair and officers of Synod.

Plymouth and Exeter District

Chair:
John Carne

Secretary:
Peter Williamson

Further Education

God of many names
whose servants worship
in different ways,
pour your love
onto the College Campus.
Enter lives
concentrating on courses,
exploring art
beautifying, computing,
performing drama, engineering
learning life skills,
Becoming, becoming, becoming …

*Further Education students
Photo by C Rushton*

As students grow and change, Lord,
calm their tensions.
Inspire, motivate,
and enable your people
to 'be here',
anointing, listening, loving
and watching for signs
of your kingdom. Amen

*Eileen Hirst, Methodist Chaplain for
Bradford College and the University of Bradford*

*Give thanks
for our part in the
mission of Christ
to the world*

day 25

Blessed Jesus, suffer us never at any time to be parted from you. In times of temptation hide us under the shadow of your wing. In times of loneliness and anxiety be to us a loving shepherd. In times of trouble watch over us with your love. Be to us at all times a strong tower and our sure and lasting defence; and this we ask through Jesus Christ our Lord. Amen

Margery Kempe, c.1373 - c.1438

Praying with Christians in the Pacific (2)

Tonga

Methodist President:
'Alifelete Mone

Mission Partner:
ed Ruth Watt

Give thanks for small island communities bound by kinship and their Christian faith.
Pray for students at Sia'atoutai Theological College as they prepare for ministry in a changing society;
for young people that they may not be drawn away from Christian and traditional values;
for the President and leaders of the Methodist Church as they seek to face the challenges of an increasingly multi-cultural society.

Samoa

Acting President:
Afereti Samuelu

Mission Partners:
th/ed Roy° and Jo Newell

Loving and gracious God, we thank you for the island of Samoa; for its culture, the land and its people. We pray for the leaders of both Church and Government, that they will be given wisdom, insight, patience, integrity and humility to lead your people in justice and peace, love and hope.
We pray for ministers of local churches and for the many Samoan ministers serving in other parts of the world. Inspire them and give them courage and sincerity so that their witness may bring others to know Jesus Christ.
Lord, give your blessing to the people of Samoa and encourage them in all the work they undertake to your praise and glory. Amen

Solomona Potogi

Fiji

Methodist President:
Laisiasa Ratabacaca

Give thanks for vibrant faith, generosity and hospitality.
Pray for Ming-ya, a National in Mission working with the growing Chinese congregation and for their full integration into the Methodist Church in Fiji;
for the healing of racial tension in the Church so that it may also play a vital role in helping to heal the sharp tensions between ethnic and Indo-Fijians in the community;
for the work of the Pacific Theological College;
for the Citizens' Constitutional Forum which exercises a prophetic role in society.

Give thanks to God for the increase of membership in the District and for vibrant worship and outreach in many churches, especially among young people.

Pray for peace, especially in the town of Portadown and surrounding areas, that those involved in the mediation process may be able to bring a settlement to the stand off at Drumcree.

Portadown District

Superintendent:
Jim Rea

Secretary:
Maurice Laverty

Give thanks for the confidence, optimism and willingness to change found in many of our churches and pray for the ministry of the new churches recently opened in Staincross and Emmanuel in the Barnsley Circuit;

following a Share Jesus Mission in August 2002, **pray** that the seeds sown in over 40 churches may bear fruit;

for the healthy global perspective in our District, that we may continue to learn from, and maintain our support for the World Church, the Methodist Relief and Development Fund and Christian Aid;

for the ministry of Susanna Brookes, our District Evangelism Enabler, and for the success of the District Evangelism Day planned for 22 March 2003.

Sheffield District

Chair:
David Halstead

Secretary:
Gillian Newton

Working in difficult situations

Lord, we pray for those whose work and ministry today
will be in places where there is no easy peace:
in Accident and Emergency Departments
dealing with difficult patients;
in communities where violent crime and drug abuse
are on the increase;
in schools where bad behaviour in the classroom
makes teaching difficult;
in prisons and detention centres where maintaining
good relationships between officers and detainees
is not always easy but crucial.
Lord, you worked each day
in places where there was little peace.
We pray for those who will go to work today
in difficult and often unpredictable situations.
Give them courage, strength, humility and compassion
and, at the end of the day, a sense of fulfilment
and peace.

David Halstead

*Give thanks
for unity, God's
will and gift to
the Church*

Europe

Secretary for Europe:
Colin Ride

> O God, grant us grace
> to receive Jesus Christ in
> every person
> and to be Jesus Christ in
> every person.
>
> *Martin Luther, 1483-1546*

*Turkey, Photo © Corel
Corporation*

Republic of Ireland

> Lord, you are patient
> and kind.
> Help us when we know
> the right thing to do
> but are in danger
> of choosing to do otherwise.
> Open us daily
> to your redeeming power.
>
> *David Range, Ireland*

Al = Albania
Au = Austria
B = Belgium
Bo = Bosnia-Herzegovina
Cr = Croatia
Cz = Czech Republic
E = Estonia
G = Gibraltar
Gr = Greece
H = Hungary
L = Latvia
Li = Lithuania
Lu = Luxembourg
M = Moldavia
Mc = Macedonia
Mn = Montenegro
Sb = Serbia
Sl = Slovak Republic
Sn = Slovenia
Sw = Switzerland

Lord,
deliver us
from the temptation
to hate and to glory
in the destruction
of others.

Stan Platt, Selby

British Methodist Districts

- dots are major towns and cities
- numbers correspond to the day
in the Prayer Handbook

Orkney

Shetland

30

30

20

9

13

15

27

21

29

16

18

6

19

25

17

8

11

22

8

28

23

14

8

5

2

1

7

4

3

26

24

12

10
Channel
Islands

Isles of
Scilly

*The Duck Race, Wolston,
near Coventry, photo ©
The Arthur Rank Centre*

day 26

Come, Light Divine, and illumine our darkness. Come, Life Divine, and raise us from death. Come, Divine Physician, and heal our wounds. Come, Flame of Divine Love, and consume our sins. Come, King Divine, and reign in our hearts, now and for ever. Amen

Russian, 17th century

 in Europe (1)

The United Methodist Northern Europe Central Conference

Bishop:
Öystein Olsen

Superintendents:

Norway
Ola Westad, Arne Ellingsen

Sweden
Ulla Sköldh Jonsson,
Anders Svensson,
Peter Svanberg,
Solveig Högberg

Denmark
Christian Alsted, Keld Munk

Finland *(Swedish language)*
Hans Vaxby,
Fredrik Wegelius

Finland *(Finnish language)*
Tapani Rajamaa

Estonia
Olav Pärnamets

Latvia
Arijs Viksna

Lithuania
Chet Cataldo

Russia
Bishop of the UMC in Eurasia:
Rüdiger Minor

There are now 82 churches of the United Methodist Church in Russia, the Ukraine and Kazakhstan (2,724 members and 30 ordained ministers).

Give thanks for church growth;

for all that has been achieved in **Eastern European countries** since the end of Soviet rule;

for Alpha courses, Discovery groups, children's camps and rehabilitation centres for drug addicts in **Estonia**;

for congregations in **Finland** extending their mission activity to include projects in South India and NW Russia.

Pray for churches seeking to recruit and train more pastors;

for ministers in **Denmark** seeking to address the problem of 'burn out' through shared ministries and leadership training;

for the developing of indigenous leadership in **Lithuania** and that the Church may be formally recognised by the Government.

Pray with all in **Russia** who fear that the proposed law on religion may cause religious minorities to become the victims of discrimination;

that the development of a Methodist administrative centre with student accommodation in Moscow may be permitted, and that the Methodist Theological Seminary may be given a state licence to enable it to continue;

for the Church's work among young people, drug addicts, orphans, older and disabled people;

for the development of prison chaplaincy.

The Conference of European Churches

General Secretary: Keith Clements

Pray that the vision and inspiration of this wider Conference may influence the life of its many Churches and create shared mission opportunities and mutual understanding.

Give thanks for the District's commitment to:

- focus on evangelism and attempt to plant parallel congregations,
- give priority in terms of stationing and resourcing to circuits and churches where people demonstrate an imaginative attempt to step out in faith,
- stand alongside the weak and disadvantaged and resource some of this work,
- give weight to ministry which focuses on outreach and work with younger people.

Pray that these commitments will, in the next two years, be turned into realistic action. We also pray that the many supernumeraries and ministers' widows in our District will always feel valued by the church and by God.

Southampton District

Chair:
Tom Stuckey

Secretary:
David Hinchcliffe

Mission Partners:
Edson° and Sammie Dube, Nonthandazo and Nozipho (Zimbabwe)

Chaplains to the Forces

We pray for chaplains to the Forces,
    often separated from home and family,
    frequently on stand-by and uprooted,
    always obedient and sent
to places of danger and desolation,
where humanity bleeds and despairs,
where individuals suffer and die.
    Grant them:
    courage to stand with those who hold back
    the forces of chaos,
    protection from the evil which can attack the soul,
    wisdom in their counsel and care of others,
and your presence whenever they seek to show Christ present
to those they meet. Amen

Forces Chaplain

Tom Stuckey and Peter Howson

Do not look forward to what might happen tomorrow;
    the same everlasting Father who cares for you today
will take care of you tomorrow, and every day.
Either he will shield you from suffering,
or he will give you unfailing strength to bear it.
Be at peace, then, and put aside all anxious thoughts
and imaginations.

St Francis de Sales (1567-1622)

Give thanks for the suffering and victory of Jesus Christ

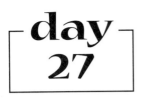

day 27

God our Father, the source from which we come and the end to which we go; be to us also the light by which we travel and the power in which we overcome. As at our beginning so, at our departing, be to us the grace by which we live and the peace in which we take our final rest; through Christ our Lord. Amen

John Hunter, 1849-1917

Praying with Christians in Europe (2)

Belgium

President of the Eglise Protestante Unie:
Daniel Vanescote

Give thanks for good ecumenical relationships.
Pray with all who are involved in many forms of caring for mission and outreach in the community;
for the further growing together of Protestant and Evangelical denominations.

The United Methodist German Central Conference

Bishop:
Walter Klaiber

Mission Partners:
p   Barry° and Gillian Sloan, Michael and Megan
p   Vanessa Cook

Pray for courage and willingness to change and develop new work;
that more may respond to the call to the ordained ministry;
for the task force dealing with the sexual abuse of children;
for Vanessa Cook beginning work with children and young people in four churches in Dresden;
for those who will carry on the work of John and Lynda Atkinson, especially the English-speaking work and the 'Drop-Inn';
for all who are preparing for the European Methodist Festival to be held in Potsdam, Berlin, 30 July to 3 August, 2003: that it may truly celebrate and rediscover Methodist values and inspire a common vision for mission.

 O Lord, you have said to us, 'Peace I leave with you'.
This peace that you give is not that of the world:
it is not the peace of order, when order oppresses;
it is not the peace of silence,
when silence is born of suppression;
it is not the peace of resignation,
when such resignation is unworthy.
Your peace is love for all people,
is justice for all people, is truth for all people,
the truth that liberates and stimulates growth.
Lord, it is this peace we believe in
because of your promise.
Grant us peace, and we will give this peace to others.

From the Waldensian Liturgy

Give thanks for areas in our District where inter-faith work helps a deeper understanding of shared roles for people of faith within the life of their communities.

Pray for the work of the Methodist Mission in Huddersfield: its new premises offer a range of services on a daily basis and its doors are open to all;

for the chaplaincy work in the new Kirkgate shopping complex ministering to shop workers and shoppers: this venture is supported by all town centre churches and Churches Together in Huddersfield and District.

West Yorkshire District

Chair:
Peter Whittaker

Secretary:
Ruth Gee

Serving the customer

Lord, today I shall meet all sorts of people
   and work with others.
Be with me every part of the day.
Give me wisdom, understanding and an able memory
to use my knowledge to meet their needs.
When it's busy and I am not sure what to do next,
give me humour and calm to diffuse difficult situations.
When I am on my own in making a decision,
comfort me with your care.
Help me, when my head is full of all that is happening,
to work with the care and accuracy that I need.
And when the day is nearly over and I am tired,
help me to offer the same quality of service
   to the last customer as I gave to the first.
So, Lord, I commit this day to you.
Help me to treat each individual
as I would want to treat you.

Ann and Rob Burridge, pharmacists, Redhill

Give thanks for the power of Christ to transform our suffering

Loving God,
   in this age of global and local acts of aggression
   committed by people of all races,
lead us in the paths of peace.
Bring us the understanding that leads to tolerance of differing views,
to justice and harmony.
We need you to forgive us,
making us open to your teaching,
that we may find new ways of peace.

Les Barber

day 28

Enlarge our souls, O God, with the gift of divine grace, that hoping all things and enduring all things we may become for others instruments of your healing mercy. In all things attune our hearts to the impulse of your Kingdom and our lives to the harmony of eternal love; that your will may be done on earth, as it is in heaven. Amen

James Martineau, 1805-1900

Praying with Christians in Central Europe (1)

United Methodist Central and Southern Europe Central Conference

Bishop:
Heinrich Bolleter

Superintendents:

Algeria

Austria
Lothar Poell

Bulgaria
Bedros Altunian

Czech Republic
Josef Cervenak

Slovak Republic
Pavel Prochazka

Hungary
Istvan Csernak

Poland
Edward Puslecki

Switzerland/France
Urs Eschbach
Markus Bach
Hanna and Walter
    Wilhelm

Give thanks for faith and resilience and for significant developments in the publishing of Christian Literature in **Bulgaria, the Czech and Slovak Republics and Hungary**.

Pray for these small churches who, with other religious minorities, fear new laws being introduced to control the opening of new places of worship, and which will deny status and privilege to new congregations.

Pray for the witness of Christians in **Algeria** among ethnic minorities and marginalised people;

for work among drug addicts, counselling for refugees, soup kitchens, youth camps and medical centres in **Austria**.

Celebrate with Christians in Switzerland the many international bodies who have a home there:
- the World Council of Churches
- the Joint WCC and the Vatican Body,
- the World Alliance of YMCAs,
- the Committee for the Study of the Problems of Social Development and Peace (SODEPAX).

Pray that their vision and longing for peace and justice may be felt throughout the world and influence the decisions of nations and their leaders.

Grant us, Lord God, a vision of your world
    as your love would make it:
  a world where the weak are protected,
        and none go hungry or poor;
    a world where the benefits of civilised life are shared
    and everyone can enjoy them;
a world where different races and cultures live in tolerance
    and mutual respect;
a world where peace is built with justice
    and justice is guided by love;
and give us the inspiration and courage to build it,
through Jesus Christ our Lord. Amen

Source unknown

We give thanks for the varied communities of faith and culture across the District and for opportunities to learn about one another and to work together through inter-faith groups, especially for occasions of prayer and celebration.

We pray for the work of the churches' Link Officers in the Black Country Boroughs as they help to build up trust between churches, local authorities and varied community groups; for all members of different Faith communities, particularly for those who feel vulnerable and are subject to threat.

Gurdwara Sri Guru Singh ab

Wolverhampton and Shrewsbury District

Chair:
Peter Curry

Secretary:
Brenda Shuttleworth

Mission Partners:
Solomona and Ana
Potogi, Lusa and
Wesley (Samoa)

God of all, whose heart has no room for favourites,
open our eyes
to see reflections of your glory
in all those around us,
and stiffen our wills
to work with all people of goodwill
for the establishing of your Kingdom
of justice and peace.

Peter Curry

In strength and weakness

Gracious God, we trust you.
We trust you when faith is strong
and we are so certain in what we believe.
We trust you when faith comes alive
and we are carried by the excitement and risk.
We trust you when faith is hard
and we wrestle with problems.
We trust you
even when faith flies out of the window
and we are bereft.
Gracious God,
known in presence and absence,
in weakness and in strength,
deal graciously with us.
In your love accept what we are
and in your mercy,
call us into the wholeness
of what you would have us be.
In Jesus' name we ask. Amen

Christine Pocock, Free Churches Secretary for Health Care Chaplaincy

*Give thanks
for signs of
renewal in the
Church through
the Holy Spirit*

day 29

Deliver us, O Lord, from all doting love and all sentimental faith. Teach us to see the world as you see it that we may embrace its pain, carry its burdens and grasp its thorns until we come at last to the dark places of our healing and our redemption; even the death of your Son our Saviour, Jesus Christ. Amen

George Macdonald, 1824-1905

Praying with Christians in Central Europe (2)

United Methodist Central and Southern Europe Central Conference (continued)

Bishop:
Heinrich Bolleter

Superintendents:

FR Yugoslavia
Martin Hovan

Macedonia
Wilhelm Nausner

Give thanks for this small, lively Methodist Church spreading the good news of Jesus Christ, 'an oasis of hope' in an atheistic, depressed society.

Pray for Katarina Nikolic, a National in Mission who has trained as a teacher and evangelist to become pastor of a Roma Gypsy community in Srbobran in northern Yugoslavia: for Daniel Naskovski, another National in Mission working with Roma Gypsies in Vrbas;

for the Ecumenical Humanitarian Organisation (EHO) which distributes aid and offers counselling to families and young people who have been displaced and traumatised by war.

Pray for the Methodist Church ministering amid suspicion, fear and uncertainty, seeking to mediate between Christian and Islamic groups and to offer help to refugees.

Pray with a group of women who began a movement of prayer for peace in one of the villages, urging women everywhere to pray in their homes at 9.00 am. each day;

for President Boris Trajkovski who is being attacked from many sides in his search for peace in this troubled country.

The smell of wood smoke as it rises straight
on a crisp winter's morning;
The sight of Roma children laughing and playing
on a snow pile beside their homes;
The sounds of a laden donkey's slow beat,
and the woodpecker's staccato rhythm;
The touch of firm handshakes in church
and hugs of welcome.
God filling one's senses with
delight and warmth and love ...
... in Macedonia.

Michael King, World Church Team Leader

We give thanks for the Institute of Community Theology in York and pray for the new Director Richard Andrew;

we give thanks for the newly signed Covenant between the Mowbray Deanery and the Thirsk and Northallerton circuit and pray for continuing ecumenical co-operation between all faith communities;

we give thanks for the historic sacred places in our District which inspire and challenge us today.

We pray for the farming communities and for the tourist industry; for Christian communities who are seeking to be church in a creative way.

When marriage ends in divorce

Gracious God,
we remember before you a marriage that began
   with high hopes.
We give you thanks for the years of joy and security
which this partnership has brought
and for the love given and received.
Now we place before you the times that have been
   impossible,
the hearts that have grown cold
and the feelings that cannot be resolved.
You are a God of healing and forgiveness
and we pray that bitterness may not sour our future
nor unresolved issues burn within us.
We pray that you will continue to bless and guide
   in separation
those who once stood before you as one ...

From Vows and Partings (Methodist Publishing House)

York and Hull District

Chair:
Stuart Burgess

Secretary:
Rosemary Harrison

Gracious God,
we thank you for Aelred of Rievaulx and Hilda of Whitby who helped to plant the faith in our land and inspired people of their day; help us to draw strength from the saints as we continue our journey:
   in our uncertainty, light up our path;
   in our vulnerability, give us strength;
   in our arrogance, give us humility
      and enfold us in your love. Amen

Stuart Burgess

Give thanks for God's faithful departed servants who have revealed his grace and enriched our Christian pilgrimage

day 30

Lord Jesus Christ, by your thorn-crowned head, receive the devotion of my mind. Lord Jesus Christ, by your nail-pierced hands, accept my daily work. Lord Jesus Christ, by your wounded feet, bless my faltering journey. Lord Jesus Christ, by your riven side, accept the adoration of my heart; for your love and your mercy's sake. Amen

After George Spencer, Father Ignatius, 1799-1864

Praying with Christians in Southern Europe

Portugal

Bishop:
Sifredo Teixeira
rt   Cora Aspey

Spain
Iglesia Evangelica Española

President:
Pastor Enrique Capo

Italy

Methodist President:
Valdo Benecchi

Mission Partners:
p   Richard°, Carol
     and John Grocott

Give thanks for ecumenical encounters and relationships.

Pray for the Methodist Church in **Portugal** as it develops new forms of ministry and seeks, out of scarce resources, to minister to people in the Portuguese-speaking countries of Timor and Mozambique;

for churches in **Spain** which, in collaboration with the State, are adapting old properties to welcome and accommodate refugees and asylum seekers;

for a new project in **Italy** to create eight flats for refugees and immigrants and for the development of understanding relationships between Italians and immigrant communities;

for social ministries, including work with prostitutes in southern Italy.

God, in your great mercy,
   you raised Jesus Christ from the dead,
   a source of living hope and power
      to all who struggle to realise your peace and justice.
   Forgive us for seeking shelter behind the locked doors
of cultural divide and ethnic identities.
Breathe into us your Holy Spirit
and speak to us of your peace.
Give to us all a living experience
of your death and resurrection.
Come to us in your transforming power.
Burn the prejudice, hatred and fears in our lives.
Help us to receive the gospel of forgiveness
and to share in that same ministry of reconciliation,
within our own shores and in the whole world. Amen

Akuila Yabaki, Fiji

We give thanks for the newly created 'Rainbow Turtle', a Fair Trade initiative at Paisley Central Hall to provide a resource for Justice and Peace and One World issues in that area.

We pray for the Synod as it learns to re-pattern its way of being together in the shape of 'Our Calling' to support the mission of local faith communities;

for the work of the Scottish Churches Agency for Racial Justice as it re-focuses its work and develops its resources to give better effect to the commitment of Churches in Scotland to racial justice both locally and globally.

Scotland District

Chair:
James Jones

Secretary:
David Cooper

God of all nations, **we give thanks** for our Viking heritage, and for all those who, down through the years, have found here a safe haven in stormy waters; that here are people with deep family roots alongside those from many places who have made these islands their home. May your Spirit enable us to rejoice together in our unique environment.

We give thanks for the new building extension to our chapel in East Yell, enhancing our work in a remote rural area.

We pray for lay pastor Douglas Graham, working on the islands of Yell and Unst where, at Haroldswick, Britain's most northerly church is to be found;

for the faithful people of our small country churches and the scattered communities in which they live.

Shetland District

Chair:
Richard Bielby

Secretary:
Sue Robinson

Lord, you are the giver of life,
in the midst of suffering, we celebrate the promise
of your peace;
in the midst of oppression, we celebrate the promise
of freedom;
in the midst of doubt and despair, we celebrate
the promise of faith and hope;
in the midst of fear, we celebrate the promise of joy;
in the midst of sin and decay, we celebrate the promise
of salvation and renewal;
in the midst of death, we celebrate the promise
of eternal life.

World Council of Churches, 1983 Assembly, Vancouver

*Give thanks
for our foretaste
of the life of the
world to come*

In living and in dying, O Lord, I would be yours alone. Keep me as your own for ever and draw me daily nearer to your sacred heart. Fill me each day with your most holy love until, by your grace, I behold with your saints the unclouded vision of your face in glory; through Christ our Lord. Amen

Edward Bouverie Pusey, 1800-1882

Praying with Christians oikoumene **World Council of Churches**

2001-2010 Decade to Overcome Violence

Give thanks that the World Council of Churches, itself a global village, is committed to developing a sense of international community.

Pray for all who work in its name in countries where there is conflict and suffering to bring reconciliation and peace;

for those who, in a spirit of solidarity, visit war-torn areas to share the suffering, hear the stories and encourage the churches;

for those who question national and international policies that not only widen the gap between rich and poor, but also exclude and fail to listen to the voice of the poor;

for all who work to overcome racism and xenophobia;

for those engaged in the struggle for human rights ...

In seeking reconciliation and peace, may we begin with ourselves, the ways we act in our own families, our community, our church, our country ...

South to South scholarships:
Rebecca Acuna Ferrerio (Cuba)
Esmel Amari° (Côte d'Ivoire)
German Chambi° (Bolivia)
Virgile Dosseh° (Togo)
Kpoti Lassey° (Togo)
Roland Mae° (Solomon Islands)
Matilda Mendy (The Gambia)
Maximo Avila (Peru)
David Ntogohnya° (Uganda)
Anil Reuben° (Fiji)
Janett Rojas (Peru)
Paulina Viucuvu° (Fiji)
U Zahmingliana (Myanmar)

Eternal God,
    whose image lies in the hearts of all people,
We live among peoples whose ways are different
    from ours,
            whose faiths are foreign to us,
            whose tongues are unintelligible to us.
Help us to remember that you love all people
    with your great love,
            that all religion is an attempt to respond to you,
            that the yearnings of other hearts
            are much like our own and are known to you.
Help us to recognise you in the words of truth,
    the things of beauty, the actions of love about us.
We pray through Christ,
    who is a stranger to no one land more than another,
    and to every land no less than another.

WCC Vancouver Assembly, 1983

Prayer for unity

Lord, we thank you for your love to all creation,
for your care of all creatures and all seasons;
for making humankind the crown of things.
We confess that we have swerved from your purpose:
we have created inequality between men and women
and between people of different races.
Give us the heart to bring discrimination to an end
and to love one another as you have loved us.
Remind us that we are made in your image.
Take away all barriers that divide us;
remind us constantly that in your Kingdom
there is no black or white, male or female,
and make us work towards this unity in all places,
through Jesus Christ our Lord. Amen

Joshua Olukayode Adeogun, Nigeria/UCA

Mission Partners recently returned from overseas:
John and Lynda Atkinson (Germany)
John and Rita Bennett (Bangladesh)
Martin Harrison and Bridget Kellett (Zambia)
Finlay and Rachel Hodge (Nepal)
Sarah Ker (China)
Mervyn and Claudette Kilpatrick (Zimbabwe)
Michael Moss (Sierra Leone)
Nigel Simpson (Nigeria)
Ian Smith (Japan)
Kathryn Thomas (Chile)
Rosie Venner (South Africa)
Susan Wilson (Chile)

Mission Partners in transit or in training:
James Crook
Michael and Maureen Hawksworth
Andrew and Sheila Moffoot
Nick Prince
Jeana Scofield
Nicola Vidamour

Lord Jesus,
when you invite us into your village, it is dusk.
What shall I bring you?
A lamp, that shines through the bamboo slats
of my silent house?
Shall we walk together down to the crowded street?
Rather let me see you in the reflections
of the full moonlight in the paddy fields.
Let me find you in the faces of your people,
sitting near their ponds,
speaking of their families, their neighbours, their cow.
Let me walk with you, through shady paths of coconut,
nim and bell trees, to where you prepare a welcome:
a home in the human heart, where you dwell for ever,
through your Holy Spirit. Amen

John Bennett, Bangladesh
Written in Dhamshur, near to where Hindus have been attacked.

Christ is the morning star
who, when the night of this world is past,
brings to his saints
the promise of the light of life,
and opens everlasting day.

Venerable Bede (673-735)

Give thanks for the communion of saints

Readings, Hymns and Psalms 2002/3

Readings broadly compare with the International Bible Reading Association's *Words for Today (2002 & 2003)*. Explicit attention is given to various 'holy days' and other special occasions often celebrated. The New Revised Standard Version of the Bible has been used during preparation. Choice of Psalms has been aided by the Methodist Sacramental Fellowship's *The Divine Office* (1975). The work has been undertaken by Philip Turner and Norman Wallwork.

Abbreviations: HP = Hymns & Psalms (1983) Ps = Psalm

Week beginning 1 September 2002:
   22nd in Ordinary Time
The Glory Revealed

S	1	Matthew 16.21-28	HP459	Ps 105
M	2	John 12.23-30	HP785	Ps 30
T	3	Luke 9.28-36	HP155	Ps 31.1-8
W	4	2 Corinthians 4.1-6	HP269	Ps 31.9-24
T	5	Hebrews 2.10-18	HP74	Ps 32
F	6	Colossians 1.15-20	HP627	Ps 34
S	7	Ephesians 1.17-23	HP547	Ps 36

Week beginning 8 September: 23rd in Ordinary Time
Changed into the Likeness of Christ

S	8a	Matthew 18.15-20	HP549	Ps 149
M	9	Colossians 1.9-14	HP551	Ps 38.1-9
T	10	Colossians 3.1-11	HP618	Ps 38.10-22
W	11	1 Corinthians 15.42-49	HP231	Ps 39
T	12	2 Corinthians 3.12-18	HP325	Ps 40
F	13	2 Corinthians 4.16-18	HP381	Ps 41
S	14b	John 3.13-17	HP427	Ps 22

[a = Racial Justice Sunday; b= Holy Cross Day]

Week beginning 15 September: 24th in Ordinary Time
The Glory to Come

S	15	Matthew 18.21-35	HP134	Ps 114
M	16	Revelation 19.1-8	HP266	Ps 49
T	17	Revelation 21.22-27	HP501	Ps 50
W	18	Hebrews 12.18-29	HP24	Ps 51
T	19	1 Corinthians 15.50-57	HP464	Ps 52
F	20	Isaiah 40.3-5, 28-31	HP663	Ps 53
S	21c	Matthew 9.9-13	HP141	Ps 119.65-72

[c = Matthew, Apostle & Evangelist]

Week beginning 22 September: 25th in Ordinary Time
The Mind of Christ

S	22	Matthew 20.1-16	HP362	Ps 105
M	23	Philippians 1.1-18	HP603	Ps 55.1-8
T	24	Philippians 1.19-26	HP752	Ps 55.16-22
W	25	Philippians 1.27-30	HP274	Ps 56
T	26	Philippians 2.1-4	HP726	Ps 57
F	27	Philippians 2.5-11	HP253	Ps 61
S	28	Philippians 2.12-18	HP401	Ps 62

Week beginning 29 September: 26th in Ordinary Time
The Life of Christ

S	29d	Revelation 12.7-12	HP592	Ps 103
M	30	Philippians 2.19-3.11	HP751	Ps 63
T	1	Philippains 3.12-14	HP742	Ps 65
W	2	Philippians 3.14 -4.1	HP247	Ps 66
T	3	Philippians 4.2-9	HP261	Ps 69.1-13
F	4	Philippians 4.10-14	HP318	Ps 71.1-14
S	5	Philippians 4.15-23	HP524	Ps 71.15-24

[d = Michael and All Angels]

Week beginning 6 October: 27th in Ordinary Time
Planting and Pruning

S	6	Matthew 21.33-46	HP322	Ps 19
M	7	Isaiah 5.1-17	HP521	Ps 73.1-13
T	8	Proverbs 2.1-11	HP32	Ps 73.14-28
W	9	1 John 2.1-17	HP693	Ps 77
T	10	Genesis 2.4b-15	HP58	Ps 78
F	11	Exodus 20.1-20	HP468	Ps 81
S	12	Mark 10.2-16	HP471	Ps 80

Week beginning 13 October: 28th in Ordinary Time
The Great Feast

S	13	Matthew 22.1-14	HP139	Ps 106
M	14	Isaiah 25.1-9	HP401	Ps 84
T	15	Proverbs 3.1-18	HP672i	Ps 87
W	16	1 John 3.1-15	HP666	Ps 88
T	17	Jeremiah 33.1-11	HP38	Ps 89.1-15
F	18e	2 Timothy 4.5-17	HP148	Ps 147
S	19	Exodus 32.1-14	HP519	Ps 23

[Week of Prayer for World Peace; e = Luke the Evangelist]

Week beginning 20 October: 29th in Ordinary Time
The Challenge of Justice

S	20	Matthew 22.15-22	HP797	Ps 96
M	21	Amos 1.2-28	HP321	Ps 92
T	22	Amos 2.10-13	HP529	Ps 96
W	23	Amos 3.1-8	HP541	Ps 99
T	24	Amos 4.1-5	HP505	Ps 101
F	25	Amos 5.4-8	HP138	Ps 105.1-15
S	26	Amos 5.10-15	HP414	Ps 106.1-9,43-48

[One World Week]

Week beginning 27 October: 30th in Ordinary Time

The Cost of Discipleship

S	27	Matthew 22.34-46	HP313	Ps 90
M	28f	Luke 6.12-16	HP706	Ps 116
T	29	Amos 5.18 - 6.6	HP484	Ps 117
W	30	Amos 7.8-16	HP454	Ps 147
T	31	Amos 8.4-7	HP314	Ps 148
F	1g	Revelation 7.9-17	HP812	Ps 34
S	2	Amos 9.13-15	HP816	Ps 149

[f = Simon & Jude, Apostles; g = All Saints' Day]

Week beginning 3 November: 31st in Ordinary Time

Gathering In

S	3h	Matthew 23.1-12	HP163	Ps 107.1-7,33-37
M	4	Micah 4.1-4	HP783	Ps 150
T	5	Isaiah 49.5-6	HP462	Ps 145
W	6	Zechariah 8.20-23	HP456	Ps 144
T	7	Isaiah 55.1-5	HP756i	Ps 103
F	8	Jeremiah 3.15-18	HP588	Ps 101
S	9	Isaiah 66.18-23	HP49	Ps 93

[h = Methodist Homes Sunday]

Week beginning 10 November: 32nd in Ordinary Time

Going Out

S	10i	Matthew 25.1-13	HP412	Ps 78
M	11	Luke 10.1-9	HP679	Ps 86
T	12	John 20.19-23	HP763	Ps 85
W	13	Acts 5.12-21	HP395	Ps 74.1-12
T	14	Luke 24.44-53	HP299	Ps 74.12-23
F	15	John 1.35-42	HP697	Ps 73.1-13
S	16	Acts 16.1-10	HP326	Ps 73.14-28

[i = Remembrance Sunday]

Week beginning 17 November: 33rd in Ordinary Time

Proclaiming the Good News

S	17	Matthew 25.14-30	HP632	Ps 123
M	18	Acts 8.4-12	HP570	Ps 44
T	19	Acts 13.26-33a	HP465	Ps 33
W	20	Acts 17.22-34	HP4	Ps 26
T	21	1 Corinthians 1.18-25	HP182	Ps 19
F	22	Colossians 1.24-29	HP167	Ps 137.1-6
S	23	1 Thessalonians 2.1-8	HP793	Ps 139

[Prisons Week]

Week beginning 24 November: Week Before Advent

Hearing the Good News

S	24j	Matthew 25.31-46	HP147	Ps 95
M	25	Acts 26.12-18	HP419	Ps 100
T	26	Acts 16.11-15	HP240	Ps 12
W	27	Acts 16.25-34	HP733	Ps 1
T	28	Ephesians 1.3-14	HP68	Ps 113
F	29	1 Peter 2.4-9	HP622	Ps 2
S	30k	Matthew 4.18-22	HP152	Ps 19

[j = Christ the King & Youth Sunday; k = Andrew the Apostle]

Week beginning 1 December: 1st of Advent

Watching and Waiting

S	1	Isaiah 64.1-9	HP236	Ps 80
M	2	Mark 4.1-9	HP433	Ps 96
T	3	Mark 4.10-12	HP466	Ps 98
W	4	Mark 11.12-14	HP668	Ps 9
T	5	Mark 14.32-42	HP631	Ps 50
F	6	Mark 8.11-13	HP667	Ps 97
S	7	Mark 4.26-29	HP355	Ps 45

Week beginning 8 December: 2nd of Advent

The Baptist

S	8	Isaiah 40.1-11	HP56	Ps 85
M	9	Mark 1.1-15	HP85	Ps 72
T	10	Mark 10.35-45	HP80	Ps 82
W	11	Mark 6.14-29	HP516	Ps 94
T	12	Mark 8.31-33	HP84	Ps 48
F	13	Mark 15.21-32	HP267	Ps 67
S	14	Mark 12.38-40	HP248	Ps 76

Week beginning 15 December: 3rd of Advent

The Holy Family

S	15	Isaiah 61.1-11	HP81	Ps 126
M	16	Mark 2.13-17	HP78	Ps 7
T	17	Mark 1.16-20	HP75	Ps 11
W	18	Mark 7.24-30	HP467	Ps 110
T	19	Mark 8.34 - 9.1	HP245	Ps 113
F	20	Mark 6.1-6a	HP143	Ps 89.1-15
S	21	Mark 9.38-41	HP349	Ps 89.16-37

Week beginning 22 December: 4th of Advent

Christmas Feasting

S	22	2 Samuel 7.1-11, 16	HP83	Ps 89
M	23	Mark 10.13-16	HP244	Ps 75
T	24	Mark 14.12-31	HP600	Ps 19
W	25l	John 1.1-14	HP77	Ps 98
T	26m	Acts 7.51-60	HP818	Ps 119.161-168
F	27n	1 John 1	HP106	Ps 117
S	28o	Jeremiah 31.15-17	HP127	Ps 124

[l = Christmas Day; m = Stephen, Deacon, First Martyr;
n = John, Apostle and Evangelist; o = The Holy Innocents]

Week beginning 29 December: 1st of Christmas

Kingdom Come

S	29	Isaiah 61.10 - 62.3	HP90	Ps 148
M	30	Mark 12.28-34	HP105	Ps 96
T	31	Mark 10.17-22	HP91	Ps 85
W	1p	Numbers 6.22-27	HP354	Ps 8
T	2	Ephesians 2.1-20	HP98	Ps 102
F	3	Romans 3.1-20	HP101	Ps 111
S	4	Romans 3.21-31	HP113	Ps 97

[p= The Naming and Circumcision of Jesus]

Week beginning 5 January 2002: The Epiphany
Christ for All

S	5q	Jeremiah 31.7-14	HP129	Ps 147
M	6r	Matthew 2.1-12	HP121	Ps 72
T	7	Matthew 2.13-23	HP124	Ps 27
W	8	Matthew 8.5-13	HP123	Ps 33
T	9	Mark 2.13-17	HP128	Ps 34
F	10	Acts 1.1-8	HP122	Ps 36
S	11	Acts 2.1-11	HP132	Ps 62

*[q = The Baptism of Christ & Covenant Sunday;
r = The Epiphany]*

Week beginning 12 January:
After Epiphany/1st in Ordinary Time
One Humanity

S	12	Genesis 1.1-5	HP335	Ps 29
M	13	Genesis 9.18-19; 10.32	HP430	Ps 66
T	14	Acts 17.22-28	HP420	Ps 67
W	15	Acts 17.29-34	HP418	Ps 87
T	16	Acts 19.1-7	HP297	Ps 8
F	17	Galatians 3.23-29	HP758	Ps 145
S	18s	Revelation 7.9-17	HP753	Ps 116

[s = Octave of Prayer for Christian Unity begins]

Week beginning 19 January: 2nd in Ordinary Time
One People of God

S	19t	1 Samuel 3.1-20	HP523	Ps 139
M	20	Acts 10.1-33	HP803	Ps 97
T	21	Acts 10.34-48	HP526	Ps 18.1-16
W	22	Acts 11.1-18	HP727	Ps 18.17-31
T	23	Acts 13.44 - 14.1	HP728	Ps 42
F	24	Colossians 3.5-15	HP281	Ps 43
S	25u	Acts 9.1-22	HP557	Ps 67

[t = Vocations Sunday; u = Conversion of Paul]

Week beginning 26 January: 3rd in Ordinary Time
The Stranger Among Us

S	26	Jonah 3.1-5, 10	HP517	Ps 62
M	27v	Leviticus 19.17-18, 33-34	HP286	Ps 99
T	28	Luke 10.25-37	HP798	Ps 106.1-9, 43-48
W	29	John 4.1-15	HP136	Ps 112
T	30	Mark 7.24-30	HP396	Ps 148
F	31	Deuteronomy 24.14-22	HP342	Ps 20
S	1	Luke 7.1-10	HP392	Ps 21

[v = Holocaust Memorial Day]

Week beginning 2 February: 4th in Ordinary Time
Forgiveness and Reconciliation

S	2w	Luke 2.22-40	HP126	Ps 24
M	3	Luk e 15.11-32	HP215	Ps 29
T	4	Matthew 5.21-26	HP748	Ps 45
W	5	Matthew 5.38-48	HP760	Ps 46
T	6	Matthew 6.7-15	HP766	Ps 47
F	7	Matthew 18.21-35	HP756ii	Ps 74.1-12
S	8	2 Corinthians 5.14-21	HP759	Ps 74.12-23

[w = The Presentation of Christ in the Temple]

Week beginning 9 February: 5th in Ordinary Time
Living Together with Differences

S	9	Isaiah 40.21-31	HP446	Ps 147
M	10	Romans 1.8-17	HP776	Ps 75
T	11	Romans 14.1-13	HP48	Ps 76
W	12	1 Corinthians 6.1-8	HP754	Ps 78.1-7
T	13	1 Corinthians 7.12-16	HP366	Ps 80
F	14	James 2.1-10	HP757	Ps 81
S	15	Philippians 2.1-15	HP739	Ps 84

Week beginning 16 February: 6th in Ordinary Time
Sayings to be Trusted

S	16x	2 Kings 5.1-14	HP376	Ps 30
M	17	1 Timothy 1.1-20	HP790	Ps 12
T	18	1 Timothy 2.1-7	HP556	Ps 13
W	19	1 Timothy 2.8-15	HP472	Ps 18.1-16
T	20	1 Timothy 3.1-7	HP283	Ps 18.17-32
F	21	1 Timothy 3.8-16	HP312	Ps 19
S	22	1 Timothy 4.1-10	HP553	Ps 33

[x = Education Sunday]

Week beginning 23 February: 7th in Ordinary Time
Pastoral Ministry

S	23	Isaiah 43.18-25	HP39	Ps 41
M	24	1 Timothy 4.11-16	HP435	Ps 103
T	25	1 Timothy 5.1-25	HP439	Ps 105.1-15
W	26	1 Timothy 6.1-10	HP385	Ps 107.1-15
T	27	1 Timothy 6.11-16	HP9	Ps 107.15-31
F	28	1 Timothy 6.17-21	HP282	Ps 107.31-43
S	1	2 Timothy 1.1-7	HP300	Ps 142

Week beginning 2 March: Week before Lent
The Work of an Evangelist

S	2	2 Kings 2.1-12	HP282	Ps 50
M	3	2 Timothy 1.8-18	HP677	Ps 144
T	4	2 Timothy 2.1-26	HP190	Ps 146
W	5y	Joel 2.1-2, 12-17	HP130	Ps 41
T	6	2 Timothy 3.1-17	HP131	Ps 7
F	7z	2 Timothy 4.1-8	HP470	Ps143
S	8	2 Timothy 4.9-22	HP533	Ps 51

[y = Ash Wednesday; z = Women's World Day of Prayer]

Week beginning 9 March: 1st in Lent
Creation and Noah

S	9	Genesis 9.8-17	HP11	Ps 25
M	10	Genesis 3.1-19	HP676	Ps 32
T	11	Genesis 6.5-22	HP363	Ps 25
W	12	Genesis 8.1-5, 15-22	HP349	Ps 40
T	13	Genesis 9.1-17	HP343	Ps 130
F	14	Isaiah 54.5-10	HP520	Ps 31.1-8
S	15	1 Peter 3.8-22	HP225	Ps 31.9-24

Week beginning 16 March: 2nd in Lent
Abraham

S	16	Genesis 17.1-7, 15-16	HP452	Ps 22
M	17	Genesis 12.1-5	HP662	Ps 77
T	18	Genesis 15.1-21	HP168	Ps 30
W	19aa	Matthew 1.1-16	HP383	Ps 89
T	20	Romans 4.1-12	HP729	Ps 102.1-12
F	21	Romans 4.13-25	HP277	Ps 102.13-28
S	22	Hebrews 6.13-20	HP689	Ps 139

[aa = Joseph of Nazareth]

Week beginning 23 March: 3rd in Lent
Sinai

S	23	Exodus 20.1-17	HP727	Ps 19
M	24	Exodus 24.1-18	HP185	Ps 15
T	25ab	Luke 1.26-38	HP87	Ps 40
W	26	Exodus 32.1-14	HP801	Ps 22
T	27	Exodus 34.1-28	HP488	Ps 23
F	28	Exodus 34.29-35	HP596	Ps 38.1.-9
S	29	Exodus 15.11-18	HP8	Ps 38.10-22

[ab = The Annunciation of our Lord to Mary]

Week beginning 30 March: 4th in Lent
David

S	30ac	1 Samuel 1.20-28	HP17	Ps 34
M	31	2 Samuel 6.1-23	HP487	Ps 140
T	1	2 Samuel 7.1-17	HP19	Ps 86
W	2	2 Samuel 7.18-29	HP38	Ps 89.1-8
T	3	2 Samuel 8.13-18	HP48	Ps 89.32-37
F	4	2 Samuel 9	HP294	Ps 132
S	5	2 Samuel 10	HP60	Ps 110

[ac = Mothering Sunday]

Week beginning 6 April: 5th in Lent:1st of the Passion
Jeremiah

S	6	Jeremiah 31.31-34	HP649	Ps 51
M	7	Jeremiah 7.1-15	HP63	Ps 88
T	8	Jeremiah 7.16-26	HP233	Ps 122
W	9	Jeremiah 23.1-6	HP219	Ps 130
T	10	Jeremiah 33.14-26	HP222	Ps 147
F	11	Jeremiah 30.1-11	HP228	Ps 18.1-16
S	12	Jeremiah 31.23-30	HP223	Ps 18.17-31

Week beginning 13 April: Holy Week: 2nd of the Passion
Jesus

S	13ac	Mark 1.1-11	HP161	Ps 118
M	14	John 12.1-11	HP172	Ps 36
T	15	John 12.20-36	HP171	Ps 71
W	16	John 13.21-32	HP704	Ps 70
T	17ad	John 13.1-17, 31b-35	HP614	Ps 116
F	18ae	John 18.1 - 19.42	HP180	Ps 22
S	19af	John 19.38-42	HP181	Ps 31

[ac = Palm Suday; ad = Maundy Thursday;
ae = Good Friday; af = Holy Saturday]

Week beginning 20 April: Easter Week
The Risen Christ

S	20ag	Mark 16.1-8	HP193	Ps 118
M	21	1 Corinthians 15.1-11	HP192	Ps 114
T	22	Romans 8.9-11	HP198	Ps 111
W	23	Job 19.25-27	HP196	Ps 118
T	24	1 Corinthians 15.35-57	HP203	Ps 16
F	25ah	Ephesians 4.7-16	HP219	Ps 116
S	26	2 Corinthians 4.7-18	HP191	Ps 121

[ag = Easter Day; ah = Mark the Evangelist]

Week beginning 27 April: 2nd of Easter
The Glorified Body

S	27	John 20.19-31	HP199	Ps 133
M	28	1 John 1.1 – 2.2	HP528	Ps 4
T	29	Acts 4.5-12	HP271	Ps 123
W	30	Matthew 5.27-30	HP773	Ps 124
T	1ai	John 14.1-14	HP820	Ps 119.1-8
F	2	Mark 5.21-34	HP395	Ps 126
S	3	Romans 12.1-2	HP727	Ps 127

[ai = Philip and James, Apostles]

Week beginning 4 May: 3nd of Easter
The Faithful Body

S	4	Luke 24.36b-48	HP208	Ps 4
M	5	Acts 4.32-35	HP764	Ps 133
T	6	Ephesians 5.25-33	HP515	Ps 57
W	7	1 Corinthians 12.12-27	HP765	Ps 68.1-18
T	8	Romans 12.3-8	HP320	Ps 103
F	9	1 John 4.7-16	HP45	Ps 113
S	10	1 Corinthians 11.17-29	HP598	Ps 128

Week beginning 11 May: 4th of Easter
The Mystical Body

S	11	John 10.11-18	HP772	Ps 23
M	12	Colossians 2.9-12	HP188	Ps 133
T	13	1 Corinthians 15.50-57	HP204	Ps 135
W	14aj	Acts 1.15-26	HP781	Ps 15
T	15	Matthew 26.26-29	HP597	Ps 145.1-7
F	16	1 Corinthians 6.12-20	HP792	Ps 145.8-21
S	17	1 Corinthians 10.15-16	HP628	Ps 146

[Christian Aid Week; aj = Matthias the Apostle]

Week beginning 18 May: 5th of Easter
The Authority of God

S	18ak	John 15.1-8	HP744	Ps 22
M	19	John 19.1-11	HP175	Ps 96
T	20	Joshua 1.1-9	HP822	Ps 112
W	21	Ezekiel 34.1-10	HP815	Ps 117
T	22	Ezekiel 34.20-31	HP67	Ps 129
F	23	2 Corinthians 13.1-13	HP687	Ps 97
S	24al	Romans 5.1-11	HP745	Ps 130

[ak = Aldersgate Sunday;
al = John & Charles Wesley, Evangelists]

Week beginning 25 May: 6th of Easter
Rulers Good and Bad

S	25	John 15.9-17	HP137	Ps 98
M	26	Micah 3.1-4.4	HP50	Ps 147
T	27	Isaiah 9.1-7	HP89	Ps 148
W	28	1 Samuel 8.10-22	HP819	Ps 150
T	29am	Luke 24.44-53	HP197	Ps 47
F	30	Revelation 13.1-18	HP15	Ps 24
S	31an	Zepheniah 3.14-18	HP81	Ps 113

[am = Ascension Day; an = The Visit of Mary to Elizabeth]

Week beginning 1 June:
7th of Easter/Week in Ascensiontide
Duties of Authority

S	1	John 17.6-19	HP764	Ps 1
M	2	Matthew 22.15-22	HP211	Ps 8
T	3	1 Peter 2.13-17	HP386	Ps 21
W	4	Romans 13.1-10	HP394	Ps 111
T	5	Ephesians 6.10-20	HP719	Ps 100
F	6	1 Peter 5.1-11	HP280	Ps 20
S	7	John 13.1-17	HP700	Ps 68.1-8

Week beginning 8 June: Pentecost
Mind the Gap

S	8ao	Acts 2.1-21	HP306	Ps 104
M	9	2 Chronicles 30.1-12	HP33	Ps 48
T	10	2 Chronicles 2	HP787	Ps 145.1-7
W	11ap	Acts 11.11-30	HP795	Ps 112
T	12	2 Kings 5.1-8	HP397	Ps 145.8-21
F	13	1 Kings 21.1-11	HP426	Ps 46
S	14	Nehemiah 6.1-9	HP308	Ps 99

[ao = Pentecost; ap = Barnabas the Apostle]

Week beginning 15 June: Trinity
Broadcasting the Good News

S	15	John 3.1-17	HP6	Ps 29
M	16	Revelation 1.1-7	HP241	Ps 100
T	17	1 Corinthians 16.1-4	HP789	Ps 29
W	18	Ephesians 2.11-18	HP806	Ps 93
T	19	Galatians 4.8-11	HP793	Ps 33
F	20	Mark 1.1-15	HP237	Ps 115
S	21	Romans 15.14-21	HP805	Ps 149

[World Refugee Week]

Week beginning 22 June: 12th in Ordinary Time
Building Bridges

S	22	2 Corinthians 6.1-13	HP815	Ps 107
M	23	Titus 3.8b-15	HP753	Ps 3
T	24aq	Luke 1.57-66, 80	HP82	Ps 85
W	25	2 Corinthians 8.1-12	HP527	Ps 10
T	26	Colossians 2.1-10	HP63	Ps 28
F	27	1 Thessalonians 3.6-10	HP716	Ps 41
S	28	Colossians 4.15-18	HP754	Ps 49

[aq= The Birth of John the Baptist]

Week beginning 29 June: 13th in Ordinary Time
Free Spirits

S	29ar	Acts 12.1-11	HP216	Ps 125
M	30	Luke 9.57-62	HP154	Ps 77
T	1	Galatians 5.1, 13-18	HP759	Ps 56
W	2	Deuteronomy 16.1-4	HP725	Ps 16
T	3as	John 20.24-29	HP205	Ps 31
F	4	1 Kings 19.16, 19-21	HP675	Ps 69.1-13
S	5	Mark 3.31-35	HP758	Ps 90

[ar = Peter and Paul, Apostles & Conference Sunday;
as = Thomas the Apostle]

Week beginning 6 July: 14th in Ordinary Time
Basic Essentials

S	6	2 Corinthians 12.2-10	HP378	Ps 48
M	7	Luke 10.1-12, 17-20	HP771	Ps 71.1-14
T	8	Mark 6.7-12	HP767	Ps 71.15-24
W	9	Galatians 6.14-18	HP180	Ps 123
T	10	Isaiah 55.6-11	HP460	Ps 137
F	11	Romans 16.17-20	HP677	Ps 138
S	12	Mark 15.33-37	HP228	Ps 139

Week beginning 13 July: 15th in Ordinary Time
Seeing the Vision
S	13at	Ephesians 1.3-14	HP79	Ps 85
M	14	Colossians 1.15-20	HP255	Ps 8
T	15	Deuteronomy 30.10-14	HP477	Ps 19
W	16	Luke 10.25-37	HP431	Ps 15
T	17	Amos 7.7-9	HP415	Ps 25
F	18	Luke 10.21-23	HP17	Ps 21
S	19	Luke 10.38-42	HP736	Ps 24

[at = NCH Sunday]

Week beginning 20 July: 16th in Ordinary Time
Open Doors
S	20	Ephesians 2.11-22	HP438	Ps 23
M	21	Colossians 1.24-28	HP769	Ps 25
T	22au	Mark 15.40 - 16.7	HP195	Ps 63
W	23	Amos 8.1-12	HP804	Ps 24
T	24	Song of Solomon 5.2-6	HP528	Ps 15
F	25av	Matthew 20.20-28	HP583	Ps 126
S	26	Genesis 18.1-10	HP520	Ps 46

[au = Mary Magdalene; av = James the Apostle]

Week beginning 27 July: 17th in Ordinary Time
A Kingdom Established
S	27	Ephesians 3.14-21	HP46	Ps 145
M	28	1 Chronicles 11.1-9	HP125	Ps 47
T	29	1 Chronicles 12.23.40	HP821	Ps 48
W	30	1 Chronicles 13.1-14	HP616	Ps 54
T	31	1 Chronicles 14.8-17	HP710	Ps 68.1-18
F	1	1 Chronicles 15.1-15	HP743	Ps 72
S	2	1 Chronicles 16.1,7-22	HP63	Ps 74

Week beginning 3 August: 18th in Ordinary Time
Succession
S	3	Ephesians 4.1-16	HP211	Ps 78
M	4	1 Chronicles 21.1-19	HP426	Ps 75
T	5	1 Chronicles 21.20-22.1	HP807	Ps 76
W	6aw	2 Peter 1.16-19	HP156	Ps 97
T	7	1 Chronicles 22.5-13	HP659	Ps 137
F	8	1 Chronicles 28.1-11	HP656	Ps 142
S	9	1 Chronicles 29.21-28	HP497	Ps 143

[aw = The Transfiguration of our Lord]

Week beginning 10 August: 19th in Ordinary Time
Solomon
S	10	Ephesians 4.25-5.2	HP134	Ps 34
M	11	2 Chronicles 5.1-14	HP266	Ps 110
T	12	2 Chronicles 6.1-21	HP485	Ps 121
W	13	2 Chronicles 7.11-22	HP536	Ps 125
T	14	2 Chronicles 9.1-12	HP500	Ps 127
F	15ax	Luke 1.46-55	HP86	Ps 45
S	16	2 Chronicles 9.30-10.19	HP809	Ps 131

[ax = The Blessed Virgin Mary]

Week beginning 17 August: 20th in Ordinary Time
A Kingdom Divided
S	17	Ephesians 5.15-20	HP14	Ps 34
M	18	2 Chronicles 15.1-9	HP772	Ps 132
T	19	2 Chronicles 20.1-30	HP661	Ps 133
W	20	2 Chronicles 26.1-23	HP438	Ps 135
T	21	2 Chronicles 33.1-12	HP817	Ps 118
F	22	2 Chronicles 34.14-33	HP477	Ps 119.1-16
S	23	2 Chronicles 36.11-23	HP409	Ps 119.17-32

Week beginning 24 August: 21st in Ordinary Time
Those who are Called
S	24ay	Ephesians 6.10-20	HP708	Ps 145
M	25	Luke 12.3-17	HP677	Ps 119.33-48
T	26	John 1.35-42	HP268	Ps 119.49-64
W	27	Luke 9.51-56	HP409	Ps 119.65-80
T	28	John 21.20-35	HP428	Ps 119.81-96
F	29	Acts 8.26-40	HP185	Ps 119.97-112
S	30	John 1.43-51	HP696	Ps 119.113-128

[ay = Bartholomew the Apostle]

Key

The letters beside the names indicate the type of work in which mission partners are mainly engaged:

ad administration
ag agriculture
d doctor
ed education
lib librarian
m medical work
 (other than
 doctor or nurse)
n nursing
p pastoral worker
rt retired
sd social/
 development work
t technical
th theological
 training
o minister
* deaconess

+ **joint
 appointment**
USPG United Society
 for the Propagation
 of the Gospel
 (Anglican)
CMS Church
 Mission Society
 (Anglican)
CofS Church of
 Scotland
EMK Evangelisch-
 Methodistische
 Kirche (Germany)
UCA United College
 of the Ascension
CA Christians Abroad

OMF Overseas
 Missionary
 Fellowship
CE Common Era

For further information

Flame – The Methodist Magazine – a bi-monthly magazine celebrating what it means to be Christian in the Methodist tradition. *Subscribe today. Contact Methodist Publishing House.*

Magnet – the magazine of Women's Network – *available from your local church or circuit distributor. Details of individual subscriptions from the Women's Network Office, Methodist Church House (MCH).*

Mission Matters – part of the Link Mailing – available from Methodist Publishing House, four times a year.

The Methodist Website – www.methodist.org.uk

Words for Today (IBRA) – reflections on daily Bible readings from many parts of the world and well-known writers.
Light for our Path (IBRA) – notes for those who need a simpler and less provocative approach. *Both are available from the Methodist Bookshop and the Methodist Publishing House.*

The Methodist Recorder – *from your newsagent or from 122 Golden Lane, London EC1Y 0TL.*

Copies of this Prayer Handbook, and a large-print edition (at the same price) - *available from the Methodist Bookshop and the Methodist Publishing House.*

The Prayer Handbook on Tape – *from the Blind Welfare Society – enquiries in the first instance to the Mission Education Office, MCH.*

Prayer Focus – The Prayer Handbook of the Methodist Church in Ireland – *available from Aldersgate House.*

Addresses

Methodist Publishing House (see back cover)
Methodist Church House, 25 Marylebone Road, London NW1 5JR Tel: 020 7486 5502
Methodist Church in Ireland, Aldersgate House, University Road, Belfast BT7 1NA Tel: 028 90 320078

CE ad BCE (Before the Common Era) are widely used – instead of AD and BC – as being more appropriate in our multi-faith society.

Printed by **Stanley L Hunt (Printers) Ltd**, Midland Road, Rushden, Northamptonshire NN10 9UA